GREAT MOMENTS IN Chocolate HISTORY

GREAT MOMENTS IN Chocolate HISTORY

HOWARD-YANA SHAPIRO

NATIONAL GEOGRAPHIC

WASHINGTON, D.C.

DEDICATION

To the more than 75,000 Mars Associates worldwide, working at sites in over 70 countries. Their commitment is the foundation of our company's culture and our approach to business every day, everywhere.

CONTENTS

INTRODUCTION

L egends, mythology, and lore surround the history of chocolate: a food and drink so heavenly that it makes us invoke the divine. Maya and Aztec religious texts describe how the gods gave the cacao tree to humans. In the modern era, we gave cacao the Latin name *Theobroma cacao*—*theobroma* meaning "food of the gods." At the root of these varied cultural traditions is joy—a celebration of chocolate that has spread around the world for thousands of years.

The rich heritage of chocolate reaches far and wide. In *Great Moments in Chocolate History*, you'll discover that chocolate has touched the lives of the ancient Aztec, Marie Antoinette, and World War II soldiers, among many other iconic figures. Explorers have spirited chocolate along on their journeys to the Arctic, to Antarctica, and even into space. This delicacy has delighted kings, queens, presidents, and prime ministers. It brings joy to children and adults alike. Recently, scientists have learned that nutrients found in chocolate improve cardiovascular function—a finding we expect will improve human lives.

In this book, you hold the fascinating history of chocolate in your hands,

A Maya vessel used for serving chocolate with a spoon made from a shell

beginning in the early 1500s and traveling through modern times. But we can't forget that the best things about chocolate are visceral: mixing, stirring, baking, and, most important, eating it! At the back of the book, 20 delicious chocolate recipes will take you on a gastronomic tour from Latin America to colonial North America to Europe and Asia, offering a modern spin on classics from different cultures. You'll be tempted by recipes for Viennese Sacher torte, French macarons, Belgian chocolate-raspberry silk tart, American double–chocolate chip cookies, and chocolate-peanut empanadas from Latin America, to name only a few.

You can experience the unusual, such as the Kuna cacao and banana drink, similar to what the Maya lords drank thousands of years ago. Or drink deeply from the rich history embodied in hot chocolate made from American Heritage chocolate. Developed from a recipe made in colonial America, this chocolate is seasoned with spices and

In the 1660s, a British earl created a recipe for chocolate blended with snow.

a touch of chili. Mix it with either milk or water to drink it the way American colonists would have enjoyed it.

All of this goodness must come with a hint of caution. It is tricky and time-consuming to turn the bitter, hard bits of cacao into smooth rich chocolate. But food scientists are coming up with startling and sophisticated new ways of handling cacao and coaxing the best out of the bean. Hobbyists, too, are beginning to make chocolate confections in their kitchens, going directly "from bean to bar."

As a plant scientist and now chief agricultural officer for Mars, Incorporated, I have been focusing on cacao for many years, and I must say I wish the gods had been more generous. Unfortunately, cacao trees do not produce beans quickly enough to keep up with the growing demand. Average yields are only about half a metric ton per hectare—that's slightly bigger than three football fields.

Mars, Inc., offered two million M&M's for the return of Edvard Munch's painting "The Scream," stolen in 2004.

Cacao pods on a farm in the Philippines.
OPPOSITE: *A cacao pod split open to show the seeds and pulp inside.*

And trees growing in Africa, Asia, and Latin America near the Equator are susceptible to being attacked by insects, viruses, and fungi.

The increasing popularity of chocolate in expanding economies, such as China and India, represent a challenge. In as little as five years, there may be far more demand for cacao than farmers can supply. And cacao is grown mainly by poor people on small farms, who lack access to the capital needed to increase production.

The good news is that the major chocolate companies have banded together to make cacao trees more productive by providing farmers with better training, fertilizer, and pesticides, along with better varieties of cacao. These steps will help the farmers grow more, higher-quality cacao and become prosperous enough to educate their children, who in turn may go into cacao farming. Hopefully, this uncommon collaboration will help deliver the "food of the gods" into the hands of all humans who want it—which seems to be almost everyone.

THE HISTORY
+ OF +
Chocolate

COUNTING CACAO BEANS

When Moctezuma II ruled the Aztec Empire, cacao beans were a form of currency. Reigning over millions of people in what is now central Mexico, Moctezuma II needed millions of beans to pay annual salaries and bills. As currency, cacao could purchase food and other goods as well as pay fines and taxes.

Merchants carried many millions of cacao beans from as far away as Nicaragua to central Mexico. The best beans were kept as currency, whereas older, poorly formed beans were used to make the frothy drink served to only aristocracy and soldiers.

So how much was a cacao bean worth? There are few records of the cost of Aztec goods, but by some accounts, one cacao bean could buy a tamale, 100 beans could buy a good turkey hen, and 8,000 beans could buy a copper ax.

A portrait of Moctezuma II, the last ruler of the Aztec Empire.
OPPOSITE: *Chocolate prepared with a molinillo, a traditional Mexican tool that froths the beverage.*

COLUMBUS "DISCOVERS" CACAO BEANS

Christopher Columbus's claim to fame may be that he "discovered" America, but he is also responsible for a lesser known achievement: He brought the first known sample of cacao beans to Europe. Columbus encountered cacao in 1502, when he and his son Ferdinand met Maya cacao traders (or hired porters, as some historians argue) in Honduras. These natives were carrying cacao beans—which they most likely used as currency—in their dugout canoes. When some beans fell to the bottom of a canoe, Ferdinand described the men as scrambling to retrieve them as "if an eye had fallen out."

This caught the explorers' attention. Columbus took some of the precious cargo back to the Spanish court, though he remained unimpressed by the beans. The court received the seemingly nondescript beans with little fanfare at first, but before long the Europeans would develop a passionate love affair with chocolate.

The raw and bitter bean "cacao" becomes "cocoa" once it is roasted and processed.

OPPOSITE: *Cacao pods and beans. The oldest known cacao beans were found inside a 2,600-year-old pot in Belize.*

1519

CORTÉS MEETS AN EMPEROR

When Spanish conquistador Hernán Cortés first set eyes on Moctezuma II, the tall, majestic Aztec emperor was at the height of his power. At their first meetings in Tenochtitlan, the empire's capital city, Cortés and the emperor shared ceremonial meals that included a decadent, near-priceless drink made from cacao nibs. Because cacao beans were a form of currency, this was akin to drinking gold today. Cortés found the drink bitter, strange, and nearly undrinkable.

Though the emperor received Cortés as a guest—and even wondered whether he was the god who astrologers had prophesied would appear—the Spaniard coveted Moctezuma II's wealth and power and ordered that he be taken hostage. The city of Tenochtitlan fell into chaos, and Moctezuma II was killed in 1520—although no one knows exactly how he died. When the Aztec Empire crumbled a few years later, cacao beans were among the treasures appropriated by the Spanish.

An illustrator's depiction of the first meeting of conquistador Hernán Cortés and Moctezuma II

1520

SPANIARDS RAID AZTEC CACAO COFFERS

While the Spanish held Moctezuma II captive, 300 of the Spaniards' servants broke into the emperor's vast stone warehouses to steal cacao beans. Inspired by this theft, Pedro de Alvarado, a greedy man who was part of Cortés's party, sent 50 Spaniards to the warehouse with orders to plunder the emperor's stash. The wicker storage bins in the warehouse were "so huge that six men could not span them," according to a 1554 account by University of Mexico professor Salazar Francisco Cervantes. The Europeans, who estimated that these held almost a billion cacao beans, used broadswords to slash open three bins and, according to some accounts, "stuffed their skirts and mantles" with the beans. Although the thieves stole a lot of beans, their loot did not amount to even a 20th of the cacao in storage. Later both Alvarado and Cortés exploited the value of cacao beans in the New World to build their own wealth.

Aztec warriors ate cacao cakes for strength and endurance.

OPPOSITE: *An artist's depiction of Cortés and his men arresting Moctezuma, making the Aztec king a prisoner in his own palace*

1544

A GIFT FIT FOR A KING

Explorer Hernán Cortés transported many things from the New World to the Old, including exotic animals such as jaguars, armadillos, and possums, as well as foodstuffs—but cacao is not included in the inventories of what he brought back to Spain. The first record of cacao being introduced as a food in Spain documents that a contingent of Q'eqchi' Maya nobles, escorted by Dominican friars, arrived in Spain in 1544, bringing cacao as well as beans, maize, and chilies. The visitors met with Prince Philip of Spain, who later became King Philip II.

The first written reference to the commercial cacao trade is from 1585, when cacao beans were shipped from Veracruz to Seville. During the next century, the Spaniards perfected the cacao drink, sweetening it with sugar and flavoring it with chilies, anise, cinnamon, and vanilla.

OPPOSITE: *Cacao beans are transported with their shells intact. During the roasting process, the shells come off and are often repurposed as mulch.*

THE SECRET RECIPE IS REVEALED

An anonymous traveler—known only as a "gentleman of Hernán Cortés"—earned a place in history when he published an eye-witness account of the Aztec's elaborate process for preparing cacao.

Servants ground the cacao beans, put the powder into basins, and mixed it with water. They then poured this mixture "from one basin to another, so that a foam is raised which they put in a vessel made for the purpose." The observer describes the drink as "the most wholesome and substantial of any food or beverage in the world because he who drinks a cup of this liquid, no matter how far he walks, can go a whole day without eating anything else."

This bitter drink sometimes incorporated special flowers and spices such as chili peppers, bearing little resemblance to the sweet, creamy hot chocolate we enjoy today.

An artist's depiction of a Spanish conquistador. OPPOSITE: *An illustration of an Aztec woman making a cacao drink. Pouring the drink from high in the air created a foamy consistency that the Aztec prized.*

"The men of Montezuma's guard brought him, in cups of pure gold, a drink made from the cacao-plant, which they said he took before visiting his wives."

—BERNAL DÍAZ DEL CASTILLO'S
FIRSTHAND ACCOUNT, PUBLISHED YEARS LATER
IN HIS 1560 BOOK *THE DISCOVERY AND CONQUEST OF MEXICO*

A LUST FOR CACAO TREES

Cacao's reputation as an aphrodisiac spread from the New World to the Old, piquing the Europeans' curiosity. Stories abounded about the beverage being consumed during Aztec wedding ceremonies and by Moctezuma II before his romantic trysts. In 1570, Prince Philip II of Spain sent royal physician and naturalist Francisco Hernández to the New World to seek out this mysterious cacao and other medicinal plants. Once there, the scientist found himself in a wondrous world of remarkable flora, including what he referred to as the "cacahoaquahuitl tree," which modern botanists now believe was a criollo cacao tree.

Hernández's own recipe for a stimulating *chocolatl* drink included equal parts ground, roasted cacao beans, and ground sapote (an edible fruit) seeds. These were mixed with maize and a little honey and then beaten with a *molinillo,* a wooden whisk, to create foam. When Europeans took to this exotic creation, the word *chocolatl* became *chocolate.*

OPPOSITE: *Eating chocolate can cause your brain to release endorphins, which also happens when you're falling in love.*

1631

CHOCOLATE AS MEDICINE

Chocolate appeared in pharmaceutical records even before coffee and tea, which had also arrived in Europe in the 16th century. This inaugural appearance, in a treatise published in Spain by Antonio Colmenero de Ledesma, recommended cacao as a treatment for several ailments, including infertility, poor digestion, jaundice, and consumption.

Scientists throughout Europe referenced Colmenero's essay. Henry Stubbe, the doctor serving England's King Charles II, wrote in 1662 that chocolate could treat apoplexy as well as "hypochondriac melancholy." In that same year, an Italian physician, Paolo Zacchia, prescribed it for hypochondria as well. These healers also believed chocolate could be used as a diuretic, an expectorant, and, perhaps most seductively, an aphrodisiac.

17th-century Catholics considered chocolate a liquid nutritional substitute during religious fasts.

Colmenero's commentary included a recipe for a hot drink combining chocolate with boiled milk, eggs, and sugar—a medicine that any patient would happily consume.

OPPOSITE: *In the Aztec tradition, drinks made from cacao were used for anything from cleaning teeth to reducing a fever.*

1635

CULTIVATING CACAO TREES

Almost 100 years after the Maya presented cacao beans to Prince Philip II of Spain, Europeans successfully cultivated a crop of cacao beans in Ecuador. This feat was achieved by Spanish Capuchin friars who tended criollo cacao trees in this Spanish colony.

Once Europeans, particularly the Spanish, developed a taste for chocolate, they began trying to cultivate the delicate cacao trees. Early Spanish plantations were founded on the islands of Hispaniola (now Haiti and the Dominican Republic), Trinidad, and Cuba, but none was especially successful. Others made similar efforts: The French developed plantations on Martinique and St. Lucia and in the Guianas, while the English planted trees in Jamaica.

Initially, the friars grew cacao trees, harvested beans, and made chocolate in the New World to ship to the Iberian Peninsula. Eventually, the Spanish king granted his country's monasteries the right to make chocolate from imported cacao beans.

A painting of an early cacao plantation in the West Indies. These plantations were owned by Europeans, though native people worked the land.

ENGLAND'S FIRST CHOCOLATE HOUSE OPENS

Much to the public's delight, the first chocolate café opened in Queen's Head Alley in London. A love of chocolate had spiked in England, where anyone could imbibe a cup of the sweet brew if they had the means. This was not the case on the Continent, where chocolate was a drink reserved for the aristocracy.

Because a cup of chocolate was expensive, several exceedingly fashionable chocolate houses had opened around London's St. James's Square by the early 1700s. Here politicians and nobles gathered to discuss the issues of the day and take part in high-stakes gaming—as well as drink chocolate and coffee. A tunnel running from one of these chocolate houses to a tavern in Piccadilly was discovered in 1932; historians believe it was created as an escape route for the Jacobites, who were probably sipping hot drinks as they plotted to overthrow the king.

OPPOSITE: *Opened the same year as the first chocolate house in London, this 1657 chocolate house in northern England is still in business today.*

1659

THE KING'S CHOCOLATIER

L ouis XIV, aka the Sun King, was one of chocolate's earliest champions. He even went so far as to appoint Parisian David Chaillou as *chocolatier du roi* (chocolatier of the king) in 1659. With this appointment, the king could be assured that the chocolate consumed by his noblemen would be of the highest quality.

In France, as in other European countries, chocolate was considered a luxury and only the upper classes were permitted to indulge. Granted "the exclusive privilege of making, selling, and proposing for consumptions a certain composition called chocolate," Chaillou opened an exclusive shop on the rue de l'Arbre-Sec, near the Louvre, and invited the aristocracy to visit. Chaillou held his royal post for 29 years and served the first hot drinking chocolate in a Parisian chocolate house.

A painting from the palace at Versailles features members of the French elite indulging in cups of chocolate.

TASTES LIKE WITCHCRAFT

In a stunning and not benign inconsistency, Spain's King Charles II drank chocolate as he watched the 1680 execution of so-called heretics—even as Inquisition officials were accusing people in the New World of using chocolate in witchcraft. It's rumored that the king, known to have been mentally impaired, contentedly sipped chocolate while watching victims of the Inquisition burn to death. At this particular auto-da-fé, or "act of faith," more than 100 people were convicted of heresy, many of them burned at the stake.

The Inquisition stretched from Europe to New Spain (Mexico), where possessing chocolate could be an indication of guilt. Allegedly, witches used it in love potions, where its strong flavor hid more sinister ingredients. Surviving Inquisition documents record that one woman used a chocolate potion to make her married lover "forget his wife" and that a rogue priest drank chocolate before mass.

OPPOSITE: *An illustration of captives being brought to the auto-da-fé for sentencing. Aside from drinking chocolate, other crimes punishable by death included sorcery and witchcraft.*

1739

BENJAMIN FRANKLIN SELLS CHOCOLATE

Benjamin Franklin famously ran a print shop where he published the *Pennsylvania Gazette*—one of the most widely read colonial newspapers—and his humor magazine, *Poor Richard's Almanack.* But he also sold sundries out of his print shop, such as Bibles, books, pencils, and fine, locally made chocolate.

His access to chocolate was a sign of the times. By the mid-1700s, chocolate had become a widely enjoyed and affordable treat in the Colonies. It was still consumed only as a beverage, as uncooked chocolate was too bitter and crumbly to eat. A thriving cacao trade had formed along the eastern seaboard of North America. Chocolate manufacturers and traders imported raw cacao beans from plantations in the West Indies to North American cities—such as Boston; Philadelphia; New York City; and Newport, Rhode Island—where they were made into chocolate and shipped to markets. The Delaware Valley imported more than 600,000 pounds of cacao and exported almost 75,000 pounds of chocolate by sea between 1768 and 1773.

Chocolate begins to soften just below body temperature, literally melting in your mouth.

OPPOSITE: *A painting of Benjamin Franklin's print shop in Philadelphia, Pennsylvania*

41

CHOCOLATE BY ANY OTHER NAME

European culture formally adopted the cacao tree by awarding it a Latin name, known as a scientific binomial. The Aztec believed that cacao was a gift from the gods and used it in sacred rituals. In keeping with this tradition, Swedish scientist Carl von Linné—sometimes called the father of taxonomy (scientific classifications)—named the tree *Theobroma cacao.* The genus name, *Theobroma,* is Greek for "food of the gods," and the species name, *cacao,* is a nod to the tree's common name.

According to historians, von Linné thought the non-Latinate word "cacao" was barbaric, but he understood it was necessary for plant identification. In a fitting twist, von Linné's own name became Latinized by his colleagues and then in textbooks so that he is best known today by the surname of Linnaeus.

Some wildflowers smell like chocolate.

OPPOSITE: *An 18th-century scientific illustration of a branch of* Theobroma cacao

"The superiority of [chocolate] both for health and nourishment will soon give it the same preference over tea and coffee in America."

—THOMAS JEFFERSON
IN A LETTER TO FELLOW FOUNDING
FATHER JOHN ADAMS, PARIS

GEORGE LOVES CHOCOLATE

I f his initial 1758 order for 20 pounds of chocolate was any indication, George Washington was a big fan of this intoxicating drink—as were other colonists. The drink became especially popular around the time of the 1773 Boston Tea Party, when many people boycotted tea and drank chocolate instead.

This Revolutionary War hero and first president of the United States often drank "chocolate cream" at breakfast. In fact, months before his death in 1799, the Washingtons received 50 pounds of chocolate, likely for their favored morning drink. According to the recently published *Dining with the Washingtons,* a cookbook from Mount Vernon, the Washingtons' chocolate cream was made with shaved chocolate mixed with warm water or milk, and sometimes wine or brandy, and a little sugar. The brew also might be flavored from time to time with vanilla, chilies, and allspice—all of which gave it a New World kick.

Mount Vernon, George Washington's home in Virginia

MARIE ANTOINETTE'S CHOCOLATE PASSION

The position of France's royal chocolatier was reinstated for the first time in a century while Marie Antoinette was the queen consort and wife of Louis XVI of France. The post was held by none other than pharmacist Sulpice Debauve, the great-great-grandson of David Chaillou, who had served Louis XIV.

In those days, chocolate in Europe was served only as a sweet, hot drink. The sole job of the chocolate maker was to prepare the chocolate drink whenever the royals fancied some. The story goes that Marie Antoinette asked Debauve to mix her medicines with chocolate to mask the unpleasant taste. She reportedly preferred her chocolate drinks infused with vanilla, sweet almonds, and orange blossoms and was known to drink chocolate in the morning as readily as she drank coffee.

An 18th-century silver pot, designed exclusively for pouring hot chocolate.
OPPOSITE: *A portrait of Marie Antoinette, Queen of France.*

A CLASSIC BRAND IS BORN

Baker's Chocolate—now a household name in the United States—was originally called Hannon's Best Chocolate of Milton, Massachusetts. Hannon's was established shortly after the Revolutionary War by investor James Baker and chocolate maker John Hannon. When Hannon disappeared on a cacao-buying trip to the Caribbean in 1779, Baker bought out the Hannon family and a year later changed the name to Baker's.

The company enjoyed rapid growth during the 19th century. From the start, its mission was to provide high-quality chocolate at reasonable prices. Generations of Baker's descendants invested in state-of-the-art machinery, expanded their factories, hired talented employees, and continued to honor Baker and Hannon's 1771 money-back guarantee: "If the Chocolate does not prove good, the Money will be returned." Baker's remained a family-owned company until Postum Cereal Company (which became General Foods) bought it in 1927.

Baker's Chocolate remains a staple in modern kitchens. OPPOSITE: *The original Baker & Co. production facilities in Massachusetts.*

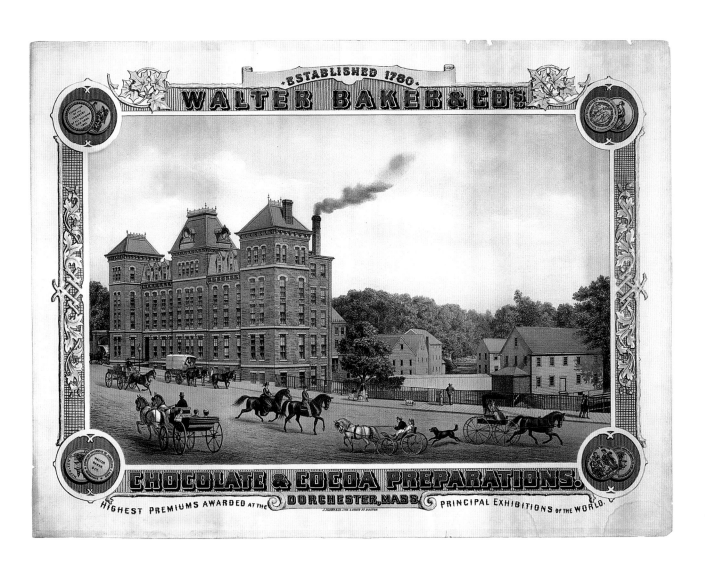

COCOA BECOMES A SEAMEN'S STAPLE

In a letter dated May 1813, Cmdr. R. H. Barclay wrote to his superior in the British military noting that provisions accorded to the Royal Navy were not being given to his men—seamen of the Canadian Provincial Marines, dispatched by the Royal Navy to defend the Great Lakes during the War of 1812. He requested that "butter, and cheese, or in cases where these are not to be obtained Cocoa, and Sugar" be among the rations issued to his seamen.

The British navy and army apparently had quite a large appetite for cocoa. By the mid-1800s, the Royal Navy received half of the raw cocoa arriving in Britain.

Cocoa was perfectly suited to be included among other military provisions like biscuits and tinned meats; it traveled well, didn't spoil, could be easily prepared in myriad conditions, and provided both comfort and pleasure.

OPPOSITE: *A British Royal Navy battleship at sea. Sailors drank hot cocoa while keeping watch on cold nights.*

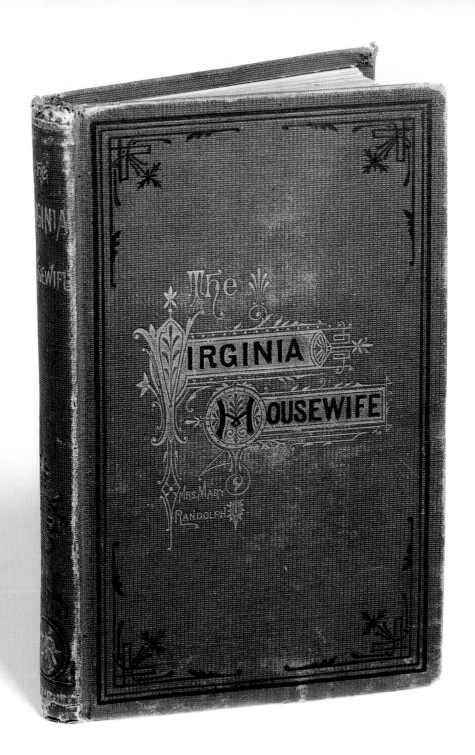

The *Virginia Housewife*

Mrs. Mary Randolph

CHOCOLATE IN THE AMERICAN KITCHEN

Mary Randolph's *Virginia Housewife*, published in 1824, was called the "most influential American cookbook of the 19th century" by food historian Karen Hess and is considered by many to be the first regional American cookbook. By including chocolate in two recipes, Randolph (a cousin of Thomas Jefferson's) indicates that it was a beloved and commonly available ingredient in early American homes.

Her chocolate cake recipe doesn't call for chocolate—it's reminiscent of brown-sugar shortbread—but the cake was to be served with chocolate. Her sugarless chocolate cream recipe was offered alongside recipes for vanilla and coconut variations as well as recipes for oyster and jelly creams, made from strained oyster soup leftovers and boiled calf's feet, respectively.

More than 80 years earlier, *The Compleat Housewife,* the first cookbook printed in North America, offered a recipe for chocolate almonds. The book was an adaptation of a popular British cookbook aimed at colonial kitchens.

OPPOSITE: *A later edition of* The Virginia Housewife

1828

THE MODERN AGE OF CHOCOLATE BEGINS

When Dutch chemist Coenraad Johannes van Houten patented the process of separating cocoa butter from the rest of the cacao bean in 1828, he made possible both powdered cocoa and solid chocolate and inaugurated what chocolatiers laud as the "modern age of chocolate."

Cocoa is made when low-fat chocolate liquor is dried and ground into a powder. To smooth out the cocoa and make it easier to mix with liquids, van Houten added alkaline salts, which yielded a mild flavor and dark hue. This kind of cocoa is called alkalized or Dutch processed. Less-processed cocoa, which is lighter in color and stronger in flavor, is called non-alkalized or natural.

In addition, because cocoa butter (fat) could now be separated from chocolate liquor (unsweetened chocolate), chocolatiers could manipulate flavor and texture by increasing or reducing the ratio of fat to liquor and by adding sugar.

During the 1804 Lewis and Clark expedition, William Clark wrote of drinking chocolate to improve his health.

OPPOSITE: *The process of creating Dutch-processed cocoa lowers the amounts of antioxidants naturally found in cacao.*

"Chocolate is a perfect food,
as wholesome as it is delicious,
a beneficent restorer of exhausted power . . .
It is the best friend of those engaged
in literary pursuits."

—BARON JUSTUS VON LIEBIG
GERMAN CHEMIST
(1803–1873)

1847

THE FIRST CHOCOLATE BAR

The first chocolate bar may have been bitter, crumbly, and sticky, but it was a game changer. For the first time, chocolate transformed from a drink into a bar that could be eaten on the go.

The credit goes to English brothers Richard, Frances, and Joseph Fry, of J. S. Fry and Sons chocolate company—third-generation chocolate makers who came from a long line of innovators. Their grandfather, Joseph Fry, had patented a water-powered machine in 1761 that could grind cocoa flakes into fine powder. Their father, Joseph Storrs Fry I, took over the business in 1787 and came up with the idea to power the chocolate factory with a steam engine. But none of these inventions would have the impact of J. S. Fry and Sons' Chocolat Délicieux à Manger ("chocolate delicious to eat")—a bar that combined cocoa powder, sugar, and cocoa butter into a paste. It could be molded into any shape as well as heated and poured over flavored centers, like fruit. The invention was a hit. In 1851, both J. S. Fry and Sons and competitor Cadbury Bros. displayed chocolate bars at London's Crystal Palace Exposition. And, as they say, the rest is history.

OPPOSITE: *A 1905 advertisement for Fry's chocolate*

1852

GHIRARDELLI OPENS ITS DOORS IN THE U.S.

Italian chocolate maker Domingo Ghirardelli first set up shop in Lima, Peru, but later traveled to California during the gold rush to sell chocolate and other luxuries to the miners.

He opened his first store in San Francisco in 1852. The company made its mark on the worldwide chocolate industry in the 1860s when an employee invented a new process for separating cocoa solids and fats that is widely used today to intensify the chocolate flavor. The products were so beloved that the company was one of California's largest businesses by 1895. After changing hands a few times, the company was acquired in 1998 by Switzerland's Lindt & Sprüngli.

Ghirardelli Square, the site of Ghirardelli's former headquarters in San Francisco, is a popular tourist destination. Named a historic site by the National Park Service in 1982, it still bears the famous 125-foot-long lighted Ghirardelli sign.

Ghirardelli employees take part in "sensory panels" for new products.

OPPOSITE: *Ghirardelli Square in San Francisco, California, is a designated historical landmark, drawing up to 20,000 visitors a day.*

Make the day with Cadburys Milk Tray*

These three are news!
1—delicious Walnut Fudge, entirely new.
2 and 3—a new look for your old
favourites Creme Strawberry
and Orange Creme

*So thickly covered with Cadburys Dairy Milk Chocolate

1861

SWEETS FOR SWEETHEARTS

Richard Cadbury, son of the company's founder, is widely credited with the invention of the first heart-shaped box of chocolates. Cadbury decorated the boxes with cupids and flowers, turning them into keepsakes. The debut of this enduring and iconic Valentine's Day product was an important event not only in chocolate history but in product design history as well.

Richard and his brother, George, ran the business following their father's retirement. While George oversaw purchasing and production, Richard was responsible for sales and marketing—sometimes creating art for the packaging himself.

The association of chocolate with Valentine's Day has been a boon to chocolate manufacturers. A 2015 survey conducted by the National Retail Federation revealed that the average American adult planned to spend about $140 on Valentine's Day, with just over half the respondents reporting they would buy candy.

An early heart-shaped box of chocolate candies from Cadbury.
OPPOSITE: *A 1958 advertisement for Cadbury's Milk Tray.*

1865

GIANDUJA GETS A NAME

Gianduja (zhahn-DOO-yah)—a heady blend of hazelnut paste and chocolate with a high percentage of cocoa butter—was first created by Italian pastry chefs during the Napoleonic Wars in the early 1800s. In response to a war-related cocoa shortage, the chefs blended plentiful local hazelnuts into the available cocoa to make up for the lost volume. The invention quickly became a chocolatier's dream, acting as both a filling, a flavoring, and a high-gloss coating for sweets.

The delicious treat had been around for decades before it received its current name at the 1865 Carnival festival in Turin, Italy. When local chocolatier Pier Paul Caffarel arranged for a traditional Carnival character named Gianduja to hand out samples of the confection, the name stuck for evermore.

Today, the company founded by Caffarel and many other chocolatiers continues to make gianduja with either dark or milk chocolate. And the European Union now has strict laws regulating the ratio of ingredients in any product bearing the name.

OPPOSITE: *Hazelnuts grown in the Piedmont region of Italy are regarded as some of the finest in the world, and held to strict agricultural standards.*

THE EASTER EGG IS HATCHED

Created by J. S. Fry and Sons, early versions of chocolate Easter eggs were made from bitter, powdery chocolate and decorated with gaudy marzipan flowers to reflect Victorian tastes. Another British chocolate company, Cadbury, introduced its version of the holiday confection two years later. For years, Cadbury and Fry vied to be the world's premier chocolate Easter egg maker, even as parts of the two companies merged.

The chocolate Easter bunny made a splashy debut in the United States 20 years later, when Whitman's Chocolates made a few as novelties. These appealed to drugstore owner Robert Strohecker, who was looking to attract customers' attention. He installed a five-foot-tall, hollow chocolate bunny as an Easter promotion. Today, of course, the cute confections have become a staple of children's Easter baskets.

Easter is the second biggest chocolate-buying holiday after Halloween.

OPPOSITE: *Decorating eggs for Easter is a tradition dating back to at least the 13th century. They are seen as a symbol of new life.*

SOLVING THE MILK CHOCOLATE RIDDLE

In the lovely town of Vevey, Switzerland, on the shores of Lake Geneva, neighbors Daniel Peter and Henri Nestlé conspired to invent a milk chocolate that was sweet, smooth, and seductively mild. Peter, like others, had been trying to make milk chocolate using liquid milk for several years, but he had had minimal luck.

That changed, according to some accounts, when his wife—who came from another chocolate-making family—had difficulty breast-feeding their daughter. Nestlé suggested they try the baby formula he had invented by condensing milk. It didn't take Peter long to realize that Nestlé's condensed milk would mix more easily with chocolate liquor than liquid milk would. Soon he had a formula for milk chocolate that pleased just about everyone who tried it. Peter formed a chocolate company that merged with Nestlé, in 1929, several years after his death. Nestlé's headquarters are still in that same Swiss town.

OPPOSITE: *Switzerland is the world's top chocolate consumer. The average Swiss person consumes about 20 pounds per year.*

1875

CHOCOLATE FOR CONVALESCENTS

When Fannie Fitch published *A Gem Cookbook* in 1875—in which she deemed chocolate "invaluable to persons debilitated by excessive brain work or violent exercise"—it heralded a succession of American cookbooks that would celebrate chocolate as a balm for the ill or indisposed. In 1901, Helena Viola Sachse published several chocolate recipes in *How to Cook for the Sick and Convalescent,* indicating that Americans still thought of it as sustenance for the unwell.

A turn toward a more modern mind-set and palate is reflected in Sarah Tyson Rorer's *World's Fair Souvenir Cookbook,* which featured recipes from the 1904 St. Louis World's Fair. In it she has recipes for chocolate mousse, iced chocolate, chocolate cake, ice cream, icing, and pudding. A recipe for chocolate fudge came in 1912 with the publication of Jane Eayre Fryer's *Mary Frances Cook Book: Or, Adventures Among the Kitchen People*.

Eating one chocolate chip provides an average adult with enough energy to walk 150 feet.

OPPOSITE: *The earliest known recipe for frozen chocolate, a predecessor to modern chocolate ice cream, came from Naples, Italy, in 1692.*

1879

TECHNOLOGY CHANGES CHOCOLATE FOREVER

For generations chocolate makers have sought to make the most tantalizing products. One pioneering chocolatier was Switzerland's Rodolphe Lindt, who invented what is known as the conching machine to improve the quality of his chocolate. The conching process is critical for producing chocolate with a satiny texture.

It begins when heated chocolate is manipulated into a paste. Then the chocolate is transferred to massive conching machines and mixed between large blades that slowly spin for 12 to 72 hours. During this time volatile acids and moisture evaporate, particles shrink, and viscosity is determined. More cocoa butter and other emulsifiers, such as lecithin, might be added to make the chocolate even smoother and silkier. The longer the chocolate is conched, the finer and more expensive it will be. Today, all chocolate is conched, making it taste very different from pre-1879 chocolate.

Lindt chocolate bunny made from conched chocolate.
OPPOSITE: *A conching machine at work. The machine was named for its original shape, which resembled a conch shell.*

1889

AN EDIBLE ARC DE TRIOMPHE

Visitors to the 1889 Paris Exposition marveled at the immense structure of the Eiffel Tower, but two more temporary creations also made their debut at the event: The French company Chocolat Menier used 250,000 chocolate bars wrapped in gold—the equivalent of a day's production—to create a replica of the Arc de Triomphe. Henry Maillard's chocolate reproduction of the "Venus de Milo," which weighed about 3,000 pounds, wilted a little in the heat and also fell prey to hungry visitors. As Professor Arthur J. Stace of Indiana's Notre Dame University described, "She shows the results of various nibblings, although the Exposition is not half over."

At the next year's Paris Exposition, Chocolat Menier wisely offered an automatic chocolate dispenser instead of attempting a sculpture. As one French writer declared, "Chocolate is decidedly not the sculptural material of the future."

A postcard from the 1889 Paris Expo shows the Eiffel Tower and the Arc de Triomphe. OPPOSITE: *Miniature chocolate replicas of the Arc de Triomphe are popular in Parisian chocolate shops.*

"What use are cartridges in battle? I always carry chocolate instead."

—FROM THE PLAY *ARMS AND THE MAN*
BY GEORGE BERNARD SHAW,
1894

1899

CHOCOLATE FOR THE TROOPS

Queen Victoria apparently knew a thing or two about chocolate's powers to inspire the downcast and renew the faint. The queen asked three chocolate companies to fill small tins with chocolates for every soldier, noncommissioned officer, and officer fighting in South Africa's Boer War, where the great British army was suffering defeats.

Chocolate makers J. S. Fry and Sons, Cadbury, and Rowntree created tins bearing the queen's image and signature and filled them with chocolate bars, but refused to put their brand-names on the tins. The owners of all three companies were pacifist Quakers and were at first reluctant to be seen as profiting from war. But ultimately they decided it was their duty to follow the queen's wishes. The troops received the tins as New Year's gifts in early 1900. Some tins were saved as keepsakes and handed down through generations—some with crumbling chocolate still inside—and are now collectibles.

A tin of chocolate with Queen Victoria's portrait, packaged for soldiers.
OPPOSITE: *British soldiers in South Africa gather for a meal in 1901.*

A NUTRITIOUS CONFECTION

Hershey's

REG. U.S.   PAT. OFF.

SWEET   MILK

CHOCOLATE

PRICE FIVE CENTS

NET WT. 1 3/8 OZ.

HERSHEY CHOCOLATE CO., HERSHEY, PA., U. S. A.

82

THE FIRST HERSHEY'S CHOCOLATE BAR

The Hershey chocolate company began as a side project to Milton Hershey's successful Lancaster Caramel Company. His newest diversion was inspired by a trip to the 1893 Columbian Exposition in Chicago, where he was so fascinated by an exhibit of chocolate-making equipment that he purchased the machine on the spot. Seven years later, the Hershey's milk chocolate bar was born.

Set amid the numerous dairy farms of rural Pennsylvania, Hershey's company developed other wildly popular milk chocolate confections, made affordable by the employment of labor-saving machinery. One such product was the Hershey's Kiss, which debuted in 1907. Hershey's Miniatures followed in 1939.

Hershey may be unique among chocolatiers in that he built a company town. In 1906, Derry Township was renamed Hershey and dubbed "the Sweetest Place on Earth." Today the township is a popular tourist destination.

Vintage Hershey's chocolate products. OPPOSITE: *The wrapper from a Hershey's Sweet Milk Chocolate bar from the early 1900s. The bar cost five cents.*

1911

FRANK MARS FINDS HIS CALLING

When Minnesota-born Frank Mars started his company in the kitchen of his Tacoma, Washington, home, he made butter-cream candy, not chocolate. A few years later, he and his wife moved back to the Midwest and opened a small candy factory in Minneapolis called Nougat House. There, Mars produced Patricia Chocolates, named after their daughter.

In 1922, Mars, who was still trying to find his niche, changed the company's name to Mar-O-Bar. Unfortunately, the chocolate-based Mar-O-Bar proved too fragile for widespread distribution. The Milky Way bar came next and immediately met with sweet success (see page 89). By 1929, Mars, Incorporated, relocated to Chicago, where improved train connections made distribution efficient and effective. Forrest, Frank's only son, also went to work with his father. The Chicago plant is still operating today. Forrest's three children own the company, and several other family members sit on the governing board.

A vintage display of Mars Chocolate Bits. OPPOSITE: *An early portrait of Frank Mars, founder of Mars, Incorporated.*

ESKIMO PIES ARE INVENTED

You never know what will inspire the next big trend. Denmark-born Christian Kent Nelson, a young schoolteacher who owned a candy store in Onawa, Iowa, had the idea to cover a brick of frozen vanilla ice cream with a brittle chocolate coating. The Smithsonian Institution reports that Nelson was inspired by an exchange with a boy who wanted both a chocolate bar and a scoop of ice cream but had to choose between them.

The treats were initially called I-Scream Bars, but once Nelson secured a patent he changed the name. Nelson enlisted the help of chocolate producer Russell Stover, and legend has it that Russell Stover's wife came up with the name Eskimo Pie.

The dessert joined the ranks of other beloved frozen treats as mass-produced ice cream was finding its way into 1930s grocery stores.

An advertisement featuring the Eskimo Pie boy. OPPOSITE: *Increased cocoa butter content in chocolate coating helps it stick to the ice cream better.*

Finest candy bars ever made

★ A MARS CONFECTION FOR EVERY CANDY TASTE

1923

MAKE WAY FOR THE MILKY WAY

Frank and Forrest Mars's first big hit was the Milky Way bar. Made of caramel and nougat covered with a milk chocolate coating, the confection became the first mass-produced, filled chocolate bar. The bar's success was the result of three years of research, trial and error, and high hopes. Although many people assume that the candy bar was named for our star-studded galaxy, it actually takes its name from a popular dessert: the Milky Way malted milkshake.

Mars bought the chocolate for his bar from the Hershey Chocolate Company and, in 1924, began selling the Milky Ways nationally for a nickel. The still popular bar, marketed outside the U.S. as the Mars bar, has held its place in the candy firmament ever since. Mars debuted the Snickers bar, named after one of the family's favorite horses, in 1930. The Snickers was followed two years later by the Three Musketeers bar.

Snickers is the best-selling candy bar in the world.

OPPOSITE: *Early advertising for the Mars family of candy bars*

1925

CHOCOLATE GETS TRADED ON THE STOCK MARKET

When the New York Cocoa Exchange was founded, a decision was made to use the word *cocoa* rather than *cacao* when referring to the beans. Away from the exchange, *cacao* generally refers to the beans before they are processed, whereas *cocoa* refers to processed chocolate solids.

Today, chocolate is a multi-billion-dollar worldwide industry. In 1979, the New York Cocoa Exchange merged with the New York Coffee and Sugar Exchange to become the Coffee, Sugar, and Cocoa Exchange (CSCE). A couple of mergers later, cocoa (cacao) is now traded on the Intercontinental Exchange.

Cacao beans are traded as soft commodities (products that are grown), as opposed to hard commodities (products that are mined). As with all commodities futures, the price of cacao beans fluctuates daily, making it difficult for small farmers in equatorial countries to count on a steady income.

OPPOSITE: *The Beaver Building at One Wall Street in downtown Manhattan, home of the original Cocoa Exchange*

GODIVA RIDES INTO TOWN

The Draps family of Brussels, Belgium, initially ran a small chocolate business from their home, but when Joseph Draps decided to open a shop to sell fine chocolates that rivaled any being produced in Europe, he was stumped for a name. Rumor has it that his wife suggested naming them after Lady Godiva, who, legend has it, rode a horse through town covered only by her flowing tresses to protest the taxes her husband was levying on the townspeople. Draps took his wife's suggestion, agreeing that the name represented a certain boldness as well as admirable values. His popular chocolate the Comtesse, which consists of a chocolate cream center coated with high-quality milk or dark chocolate, celebrates the lady of the legend.

By 1958, Draps had opened a shop on the rue St.-Honoré in Paris; a decade later, Godiva expanded into the Philadelphia and New York City markets. Today, Godiva products are sold all over the world.

A Godiva chocolate shop in Brussels, Belgium.
Many of Godiva's original products are still sold today.

1936

CHOCOLATE PUDDING IN AN INSTANT!

When General Foods introduced an instant pudding made by adding milk to purchased powder, it was an immediate hit. The company—already known for its Jell-O gelatin products—soon expanded its instant-pudding line to include vanilla, tapioca, coconut, butterscotch, rice pudding, and pistachio flavors.

The pudding was more than just a sweet treat; it was a reflection of changes in American society. The availability and affordability of home refrigerators had opened up a whole new world of food possibilities. In 1921, U.S. manufacturers produced only 5,000 mechanical refrigerators, but by the late 1930s, almost six million mechanical refrigerators rolled off the line annually. Instant pudding was also part of the new American trend in convenience food, which showed astronomical growth as the century progressed.

Each year Americans eat an average of 11 pounds of chocolate per person.

OPPOSITE: *An early Jell-O advertisement from the 1920s*

1935

AMELIA EARHART DRINKS CHOCOLATE IN FLIGHT

When Amelia Earhart felt a little chilly flying solo over the Pacific Ocean, she poured some hot chocolate from a thermos and, according to her reminiscences of the 2,408-mile flight, she enjoyed the chocolate, the view, and the peace. A few months later the aviator appeared before an admiring crowd, who raptly listened to her descriptions of snacking on tomato juice, candy bars, and malted milk tablets.

English explorer Ernest Shackleton, who led expeditions to Antarctica in the early 20th century, was also a chocolate fan. When Shackleton and his men spent the Christmas of 1902 in the hostile landscape, they shared the chocolate that had traveled with them. Shackleton took a tin of Rowntree's Elect Cocoa along on his 1907 expedition to Antarctica. The tin was discovered in 1958, still in perfect condition in the explorer's abandoned hut.

OPPOSITE: *Amelia Earhart climbs into the cockpit of her plane.*

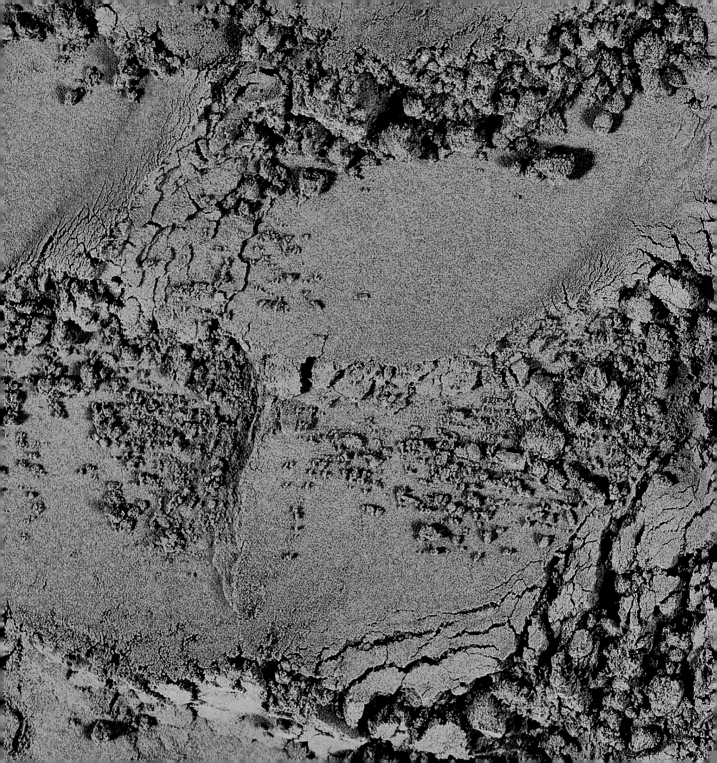

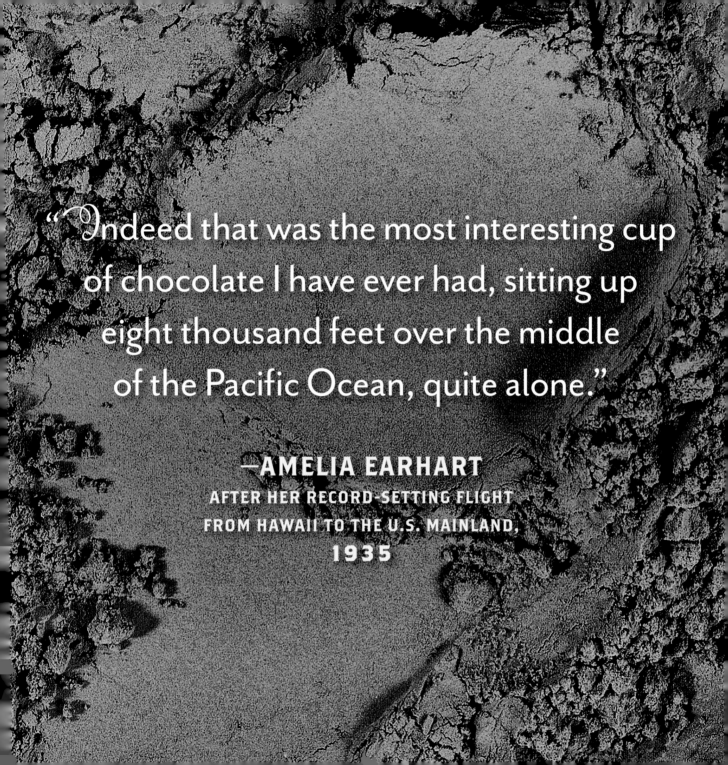

"Indeed that was the most interesting cup of chocolate I have ever had, sitting up eight thousand feet over the middle of the Pacific Ocean, quite alone."

—AMELIA EARHART
AFTER HER RECORD-SETTING FLIGHT
FROM HAWAII TO THE U.S. MAINLAND,
1935

THE FIRST TOLL HOUSE CHOCOLATE CHIP COOKIES

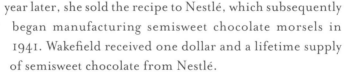

Ruth Wakefield and her husband owned the Toll House Inn in Massachusetts. One day, she decided to bake a batch of chocolate chip cookies to serve alongside ice cream. In those days, cookies were an afterthought, and though Wakefield probably never dreamed her Toll House chocolate chip cookies would be a sensation, she included a recipe for them in her cookbook, *Toll House Tried and True Recipes*. A

year later, she sold the recipe to Nestlé, which subsequently began manufacturing semisweet chocolate morsels in 1941. Wakefield received one dollar and a lifetime supply of semisweet chocolate from Nestlé.

While no one knows exactly how Wakefield came up with the recipe, stories abound: Did she run out of nuts and substitute chopped chocolate? Did she "accidentally" drop some chopped chocolate into the batter? These are unlikely scenarios, given that Wakefield was a skilled baker. But the fact that her cookies are one of the best ways invented to showcase bittersweet or semisweet chocolate chips is uncontested.

Ruth Wakefield's Toll House Tried and True *cookbook.* OPPOSITE: *The chocolate chip cookie is a winner—53 percent of Americans say it's their favorite type of cookie.*

1940

WWII SOLDIERS SNACK ON M&M'S

The story of M&M's begins with Forrest Mars, whose father founded the Mars candy company. The younger Mars had moved to the United Kingdom, where he opened a confectionery business before the war, and then began making Mars bars for British troops.

He came up with the idea for M&M's while abroad in the 1930s during the Spanish Civil War. Mars had a eureka moment when he noticed soldiers eating tiny balls of chocolate covered with a hard sugar shell. The coating kept the chocolates from melting! Mars returned to the U.S. and started making the candies with help from the Hershey Company's chief executive's son, Bruce Murrie. The M's on the candy shell stand for Mars and Murrie.

The candies were packed in the soldiers' food rations. When the soldiers returned home, they wanted more M&M's. By the late 1950s, M&M's were a household name.

A 1987 advertisement for M&M's refers back to their World War II origins.
OPPOSITE: *The M&M's slogan "Melts in your mouth, not in your hand" has been used since 1954.*

POW CARE PACKAGES INCLUDE CHOCOLATE

Scottish airman John Bremner was captured by the Germans in June 1940 and taken to a POW camp in Bavaria in 1941, where the Germans provided only "a quarter of a pint of very watery soup for lunch and 1 loaf of 'black bread' [at] 5:00 in the evening." Fortunately, about a year after he was shot down, Bremner and the other prisoners of war started getting two-person packages from the British Red Cross that contained tea, sugar, sweets, chocolate, and condensed milk. After another year passed, they also began receiving packages from the Canadian Red Cross with "a large bar of chocolate" as well as butter, sugar, coffee, biscuits, sweets, powdered milk, and cigarettes.

The International Committee of the Red Cross in Geneva, Switzerland, coordinated the distribution of packages from its affiliates. By the war's end in 1945, more than 100 million food parcels had been assembled and distributed.

OPPOSITE: *American soldiers also received chocolate in their rations. Here they pass out treats to children in France.*

You know the wonderful cakes you make
with Swans Down Instant Cake Mix...

Now discover Swans Down's glorious

Devil's Food Mix!

Shut your eyes and think of the most utterly luscious devil's food cake you ever tasted . . tender, moist, close-textured, deeply, darkly chocolate-rich!

You *still* won't know how ecstatically good your first cake will be with Swans Down's new Devil's Food Mix!

For here's chocolate flavor that comes *only* from Walter Baker's special new blend . . and a new formula that holds in all that extra-lush chocolate taste and fragrance in spite of oven heat.

Just as in Swans Down's famous all-variety Instant Cake Mix, egg whites with delicate, spring-fresh flavor are *right in* the Mix.

And this new Devil's Food Mix has the same pure, all-vegetable shortening with flour milled by Swans Down especially for this Mix.

You should hear the raves—from blue-ribbon cakemakers and happy brides—from admiring husbands and astonished party guests!

P. S. For your own favorite recipes, always use Swans Down Cake Flour. More women choose Swans Down than all other packaged cake flours put together.

SWANS DOWN DEVIL'S FOOD LAYER CAKE
(So easy! Just add milk, beat and bake!)
1 package Swans Down Devil's Food Mix
1¼ cups milk

Follow directions on box. Quicker than it takes to tell, your beautiful smooth batter will be ready for the pans.

And what gorgeous layers you'll take out of the oven—tender, light, and delicate. You just can't get such Swans Down-wonderful cake with any other mix!

Swans Down Cake Flour and Cake Mixes
are products of General Foods

**Complete! Just add milk...
No expensive eggs!**

Nothing to add but milk with Swans Down Cake Mixes! Egg whites with delicate, spring-fresh flavor are *right in* the Mix. No other cake mix contains these same wonderful egg whites. You'll soon learn to recognize Swans Down's fresh, delicate flavor.

Now—2 Swans Down-wonderful cake mixes

1948

CHOCOLATE CAKE MIX CATCHES ON

When Pillsbury introduced the first chocolate cake mix, the company barely had time to gain traction before its competitors jumped into the ring. Duncan Hines released its Three Star Surprise Mix, which let the home cook bake a white, yellow, or chocolate cake from the same box and quickly accounted for almost half of the market share.

Cake mixes had been around since the 1920s, but had not been widely distributed. One of the earliest cake mixes was for Duff's gingerbread, which used a combination of dehydrated ingredients—a clever way of using up the company's surplus of molasses—that was eventually patented in 1933. Duff's next patent for a dry cake mix used fresh eggs and was awarded in 1935.

By 1950, more than 200 companies—including Duncan Hines, Pillsbury, and Betty Crocker—flooded the market with boxed mixes, introducing a new era in cakemaking.

In 1947, Canadian kids went on strike after the price of a chocolate bar jumped from five to eight cents.

OPPOSITE: *A 1950 advertisement promotes the ease of baking at home with cake mixes.*

1950

PRESIDENT TRUMAN'S CHOCOLATE HUNT

When President Harry Truman flew to Wake Island in the Pacific to relieve General Douglas MacArthur of duty, his plane's first fueling stop was San Francisco. The president sent aide Charles Murphy into the city in search of See's Candies for chocolates, which he knew Mrs. MacArthur liked. Murphy returned with five one-pound boxes—not what the commander in chief had in mind. When the plane landed in Honolulu, Murphy was dispatched to find one five-pound box. This time, he was successful.

See's was founded in 1921 by Charles See, who relied on his mother's recipes and enlisted both his mother and his wife to run the business with him. See's Candies, which included a line of chocolates, flourished in Southern California, expanding to San Francisco by 1936. Berkshire Hathaway bought See's Candies in 1972. Today more than 200 See's Candies shops can be found throughout the West.

A box of See's Candies. OPPOSITE: *President Harry Truman greets the crowd as he steps off* Air Force One.

"Tenzing buried a little bit of chocolate and some sweets in the snow, which are really a gesture to the gods which the Sherpas believe flit around Everest on all occasions."

—SIR EDMUND HILLARY
RECALLS EVENTS AT THE SUMMIT OF MOUNT EVEREST,
WHICH HE CLIMBED WITH SHERPA TENZING NORGAY,
1953

1960

HORROR MOVIE MAGIC

In the famous shower scene in Alfred Hitchcock's 1960 movie *Psycho*, Janet Leigh's blood was actually made from Bosco chocolate syrup. A New Jersey doctor invented the syrup in 1928 to mix into milk, but Hitchcock found a more gruesome use for the product. Because *Psycho* was shot in black and white, the consistency and contrast of the syrup mattered more than the color. The makeup artist decided that thick chocolate syrup would look more realistic than the thinner "stage blood" that was typically used. Previously he had used Hershey's syrup, which came in a tin can. But Bosco's newfangled plastic squeeze bottle opened up even more possibilities for how it could be used on a movie set.

Since the advent of color film, chocolate took a backseat to recipes for red blood, many using a base of corn syrup and red food coloring. But in some cases, chocolate syrup is still used to thicken the fake blood, or as an edible mixture when an actor pretends to cough up blood.

OPPOSITE: *Alfred Hitchcock on the set of his famous film* Psycho

NUTELLA IS *BELLA*

On a warm day in Italy in April, Nutella made its debut—the brainchild of Michele Ferrero, who had inherited the family chocolate company from his father, Pietro, in 1949. The senior Ferrero, who owned a bakery in the Piedmont, had developed a hazelnut-cocoa paste as a way to stretch wartime cocoa rations in the 1940s. More of a confection than the traditional gianduja, it didn't catch on until his son transformed it into a sweet spread. The original version of Nutella was sold as a loaf of gianduja that was sliced for sandwiches. The younger Ferrero had the idea to turn it into a paste and sell it in jars. Now Ferrero buys a quarter of the world's supply of hazelnuts.

While Nutella is not the only product Ferrero produces, it's the most beloved. Another favorite is the Ferrero Rocher, a gold foil–wrapped, irregularly round chocolate filled with a crunchy hazelnut center.

Nutella's name comes from the English word "nut" and the Latin suffix meaning "sweet," ella.

OPPOSITE: *February 5 has been named World Nutella Day.*

CHARLIE ENTERS THE CHOCOLATE FACTORY

As a child, children's book author Roald Dahl was fascinated by the oversize machines that continuously stirred and folded thick, molten chocolate. He grew up during the 1920s, when England's two largest chocolate companies, Cadbury and Rowntree, sent new products to schools for feedback from kids. The two companies were highly competitive and struggled to keep their creations secret. It's easy to see how this chocolate rivalry was the perfect inspiration for a children's book in which a level-headed boy named Charlie Bucket improbably wins a tour of the eccentric Willy Wonka's fantastical chocolate factory.

Charlie and the Chocolate Factory, which was Dahl's second children's book (following *James and the Giant Peach*), has been a best seller since it was published more than 50 years ago. The book has been turned into two movies: a 1971 movie starring Gene Wilder and a 2005 movie starring Johnny Depp.

OPPOSITE: *In the 1971 film adaptation, Willy Wonka's chocolate river was made from real chocolate and cream that spoiled during filming.*

"No other factory in the world mixes its chocolate by waterfall! But it's the only way to do it properly! The only way!"

—WILLY WONKA
IN ROALD DAHL'S *CHARLIE AND THE CHOCOLATE FACTORY*, 1964

AMOS GETS FAMOUS

Wally Amos started out as an entertainment agent with many famous friends. When he decided to open a chocolate chip cookie shop on Sunset Boulevard in Los Angeles, celebrities such as Marvin Gaye helped provide funding. He called his cookies Famous Amos and quickly gained a large following, even becoming recognizable after putting his own image on the packaging. By 1982, sales soared to $12 million. His brand became so iconic that the Smithsonian added Amos's hat and shirt to its advertising collection. And former U.S. president Ronald Reagan presented him with an Award for Entrepreneurial Excellence in 1986.

Declining sales forced Amos to sell his the company to investors in 1988, who eventually sold the brand to Keebler, After spending several years down on his luck, Amos returned to working with Keebler as a pitch man for the product. In 2014, he launched a new line of cookies, called the Cookie Kahuna.

A Famous Amos cookie tin in the shape of a van featured Wally Amos's smiling face on the side.

1977

MORE PRODUCTIVE CACAO TREES

A plant scientist named Homero Castro came up with a big idea to save the Ecuadorian cacao crop, which was being decimated by a devastating disease known as witches' broom that was bringing financial ruin to many cacao farmers. It took 12 years, but in 1977, he succeeded by producing a tree he called Colección Castro Naranjal 51. The 51 stands for the number of crosses made to create the tree.

The trees were indeed immune to blight and produced about four times as many cacao beans as other varieties, but the world's cacao buyers balked after tasting Castro's "miracle bean." Gary Guittard of Guittard Chocolate described the flavor as "rusty nails." Others had similar reactions, calling the taste bitter, astringent, and reminiscent of wood shavings. However, the beans are growing in popularity as consumers learn to appreciate the taste. Castro passed away in 1988, but efforts continue to adjust the fermenting process and taste of CCN 51.

Cacao trees can live to be 200 years old, but they produce marketable cacao beans for only 25 years.

OPPOSITE: *Healthy cacao pods grow on a tree. Research into the genetics of the cacao plant could change how cacao is farmed around the world.*

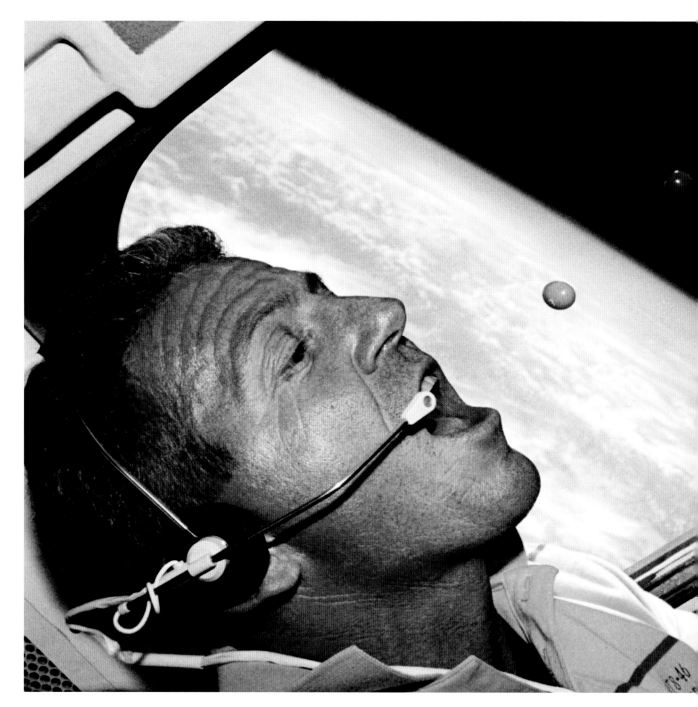

M&M'S
IN SPACE

T he space shuttle *Columbia*'s first mission in 1981 was short, but even so, Commander John Young and pilot Robert Crippen didn't want to be without chocolate that long. They asked that M&M's be included in their rations for the two-day, record-setting voyage. Since then, M&M's have been a staple of astronaut rations.

In 1996, astronaut Shannon Lucid spent 179 days aboard the Russian space station *Mir*. While orbiting Earth, she was asked by a reporter, "What do you miss?" Lucid, having just finished her last bag of the chocolates, remarked, "I would really like some M&M's." She wasn't the only one. So many astronauts have requested M&M's that they are part of the NASA space food system and on the International Space Station's menu. They've even made it into the Space Food Hall of Fame and a space food exhibit at the National Air and Space Museum in Washington, D.C.

NASA astronaut Loren Shriver shows off the effects of weightlessness on M&M's aboard the space shuttle Atlantis *in 1992.*

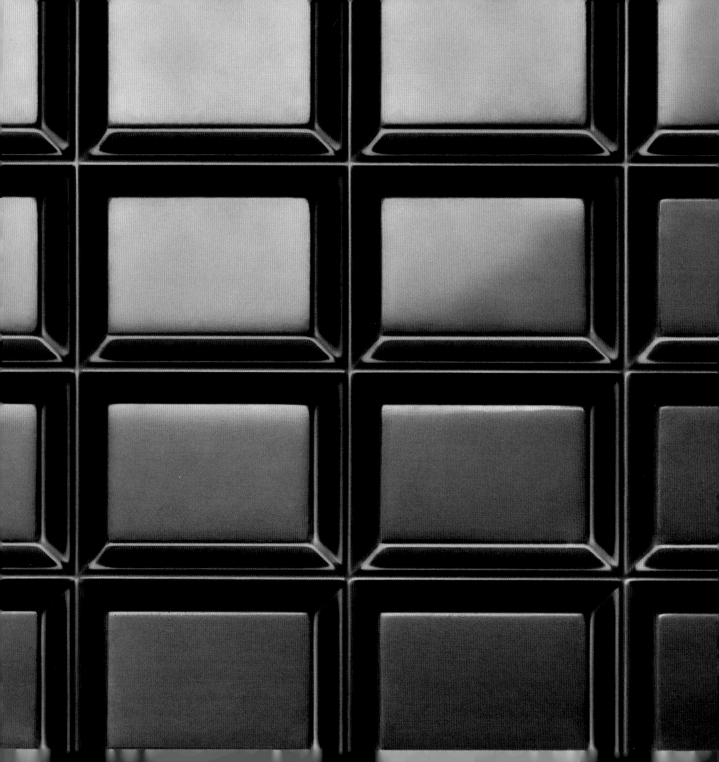

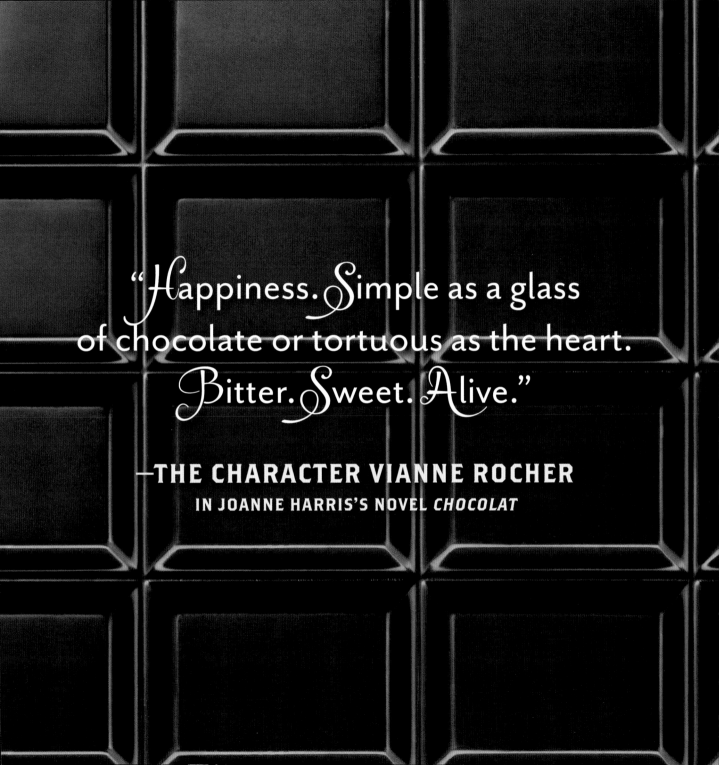

"Happiness. Simple as a glass of chocolate or tortuous as the heart. Bitter. Sweet. Alive."

—THE CHARACTER VIANNE ROCHER
IN JOANNE HARRIS'S NOVEL *CHOCOLAT*

A PRESIDENTIAL BAKE-OFF

Former first lady, secretary of state, and U.S. presidential candidate Hillary Clinton once quipped that, after her husband won the governor's race in Arkansas, she had not wanted to "stay home and bake cookies." In a good-humored response, the editors at *Family Circle* magazine proposed a 1992 cookie bake-off between the presidential candidates' wives and exhorted readers to "Bake. Taste. Vote!"

Both Clinton and Barbara Bush submitted chocolate chip cookie recipes. (Margot Perot, wife of the independent candidate, declined to participate.) Bush's recipe, which used butter, vied unsuccessfully against Clinton's recipe, which employed shortening and an increasingly popular ingredient: oatmeal. Clinton won again in 1996 with the same recipe, beating Elizabeth Dole's Pecan Roll Cookies. More recently, Michelle Obama's White and Dark Chocolate Chip Cookie beat Ann Romney's M&M's Cookies by fewer than 300 out of 9,000 votes.

All told, seven of the twelve Presidential Cookie Bake-Off recipes have included chocolate—and five of the six winners made their way to the White House.

OPPOSITE: *During the 1992 U.S. presidential election, then first lady Barbara Bush and soon to be first lady Hillary Clinton share a moment at the White House.*

1997

FROM BEAN TO BAR

Scharffen Berger Chocolate Maker, a small San Francisco business, made a big splash as America's first bean-to-bar chocolate company in more than 50 years. Because making chocolate is an expensive and complicated process, most chocolatiers don't start from scratch. But a growing number of artisan chocolatiers are crafting exquisite chocolates from the finest chocolate they can buy. They search the world for the best beans and work directly with farmers.

Scharffen Berger also labels its bars with the percentage of chocolate liquor (sometimes labeled as cacao or even cocoa). These labels have been used in Europe for years, but they are relatively new to the United States. If a chocolate bar is listed as having 71 percent chocolate liquor, then the remaining 29 percent is primarily sugar. The higher the percentage of cacao, the more bitter the chocolate. (See page 177 for more information about selecting chocolate.)

To'ak Chocolate company uses beans from the Ecuadorian rain forest to craft bars sold for $260 apiece.

OPPOSITE: *Scharffen Berger labels showcase the percentage of cacao in their chocolates.*

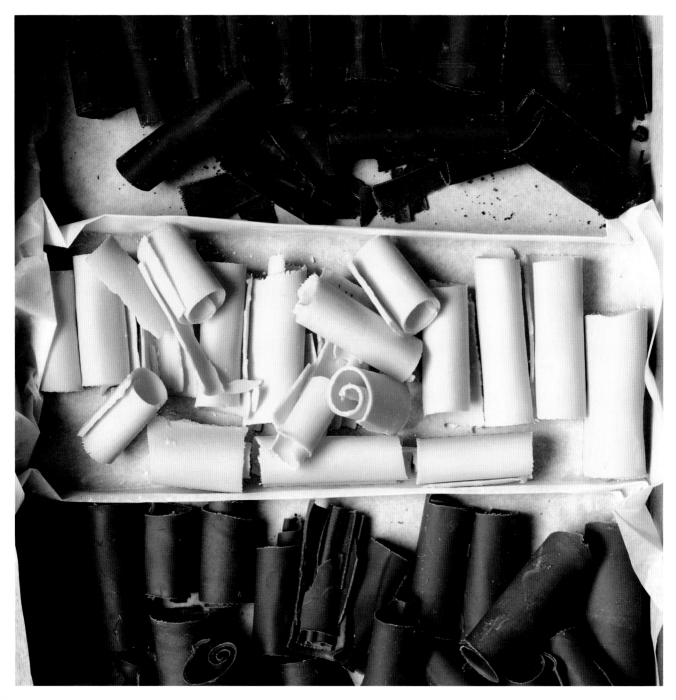

2004

WHITE CHOCOLATE IS OFFICIALLY CHOCOLATE

White chocolate is no longer the neglected sibling of dark and milk chocolate. As of January 1, 2004, the U.S. Food and Drug Administration's Standards of Identity recognize it as chocolate. Before then, it was illegal for manufacturers of white chocolate to label their product as chocolate, because the sweet, ivory-colored confection contained no chocolate liquor (unsweetened chocolate). White chocolate does contain cocoa butter, though, which is presented in combination with sugar, milk solids, emulsifiers, and flavorings to give it a whiff of "the real thing."

The change took place as a result of petitions filed with the FDA by both Hershey Foods Corporation and the U.S. Chocolate Manufacturers Association. To be called chocolate, the product must contain a minimum of 20 percent cocoa butter and 14 percent milk solids, among other standards.

A white chocolate–coated replica of the White House. OPPOSITE: *Dark, white, and milk chocolates are all finally on the same footing.*

2009

SUSTAINABILITY GETS SOME TEETH

As concern heightens over how to feed the growing demand for chocolate, it has become good business to implement sustainable practices. In 2009, Mars, Incorporated, joined Rainforest Alliance, UTZ, and Fairtrade International to lead a global effort to certify sustainability. The NGO ISEAL Alliance develops standards for evaluating companies' practices, looking at the entire supply chain. The same year, Mars, Incorporated, made the bold statement that its entire cocoa supply chain would be certified sustainable by 2020.

To qualify for certification, companies train cacao farmers in agronomy (the science and technology of growing food), provide access to improved planting material, pay farmers a premium for their harvest, and help stabilize the rural farming sector. Communities benefit because farmers can monitor environmental conditions and ensure the sustainability of their crops.

While the certification system is not perfect, farmers, governments, and the chocolate industry keep working together to make improvements. The future looks more sustainable every day.

Cacao farmers own the Divine Chocolate company. OPPOSITE: *A worker dries cacao beans in the Dominican Republic.*

"Always serve too much hot fudge sauce on hot fudge sundaes. It makes people overjoyed, and puts them in your debt."

—JUDITH OLNEY
THE JOY OF CHOCOLATE

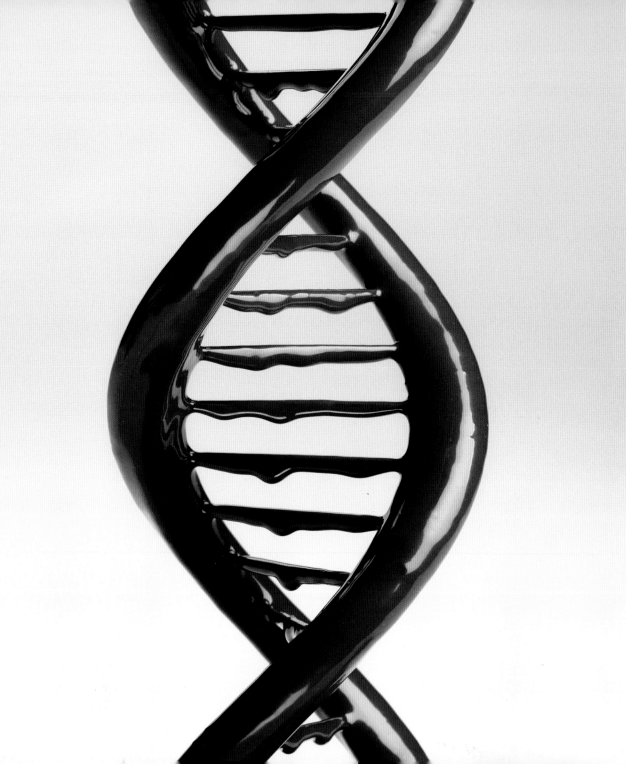

THE CHOCOLATE GENOME DECODED

Can chocolate get any better? Apparently scientists at Mars, Incorporated, IBM, USDA-ARS, and three universities believe it can. In an uncommon collaboration of industries and educators, the group released the genome sequence for *Theobroma cacao* in September 2010, and made it available to the public. They hope their work on sequencing the genome will enable the world's cacao farmers to grow high-yielding, disease-resistant trees that produce cacao beans with far less acidity than ever before.

Scientists plan to use the genetic markers in conjunction with traditional breeding so that the resulting cacao trees will be true to their current genetic makeup. They predict an increase in the world's cacao yield by 300 percent as well as better-tasting chocolate.

Demand for chocolate is increasingly popular in countries such as India and China. Mars estimates that by 2020 the world's demand will increase by about 25 percent of current annual production. These advances can't come fast enough.

OPPOSITE: *Since the double-helix structure of DNA was discovered in 1953, scientists have decoded the genomes of many animals and plants, including cacao.*

2014

CHOCOLATE FOR THE FUTURE

Twelve of the world's largest chocolate companies signed an agreement with the governments of Côte d'Ivoire and Ghana in 2014 to work toward making cacao farming sustainable. Côte d'Ivoire and its neighbor Ghana are the largest cacao-producing countries in the world—representing about 55 percent of the world's market. The companies involved include Mars, Barry Callebaut, Hershey, and Nestlé. This uncommon alliance, known as CocoaAction and coordinated by the World Cocoa Foundation, is committed to building strong, prosperous, and stable communities in cacao-growing regions and to supporting sustainable farming practices that will enable farmers to diversify and grow healthier trees. It also supports education for children and promotes female-owned and -operated farms. The goal is that by 2020 more than 200,000 Ivorian and 100,000 Ghanaian cacao farmers will be on their way to sustainable operations—beneficial for them and the world's cacao supply. CocoaAction hopes to launch similar programs in other cacao-producing countries too.

Ghanaian blacksmith Tetteh Quashie, who popularized cacao agriculture, is considered a national hero.

OPPOSITE: *Children on a cacao farm in Côte d'Ivoire*

CHOCOLATE RECIPES & COOKING TIPS

Chocolate Brownies

Early in the 20th century, recipes for the brownie, a newfangled dessert that was a cross between a cookie and a cake, started appearing in cookbooks and on bakery and hotel menus in the United States. The states of Maine, Illinois, and Massachusetts all lay claim to its invention, but no one knows the origins of this favorite. Perhaps one reason for the popularity of this thick, fudgy, chewy, and chocolaty version is its easy, one-bowl preparation.

Americans spend $20 billion a year on chocolate.

Softened butter and flour, for the pan

1¼ cups (165 g) unbleached all-purpose flour

¼ teaspoon baking soda

¼ teaspoon table salt

½ cup (115 g) unsalted butter

5 ounces (140 g) semisweet chocolate (about 55 percent cacao), coarsely chopped

½ cup (100 g) packed light brown sugar

⅓ cup (65 g) granulated sugar

2 tablespoons golden syrup, light corn syrup, or honey

1 teaspoon vanilla extract

2 large eggs, at room temperature

1 cup (115 g) coarsely chopped walnuts or pecans

1. Position a rack in the center of the oven and preheat the oven to 350°F (180°C). Lightly butter the inside of an 8-inch (20-cm) square baking pan. Fold a 14-inch (35.5-cm) length of aluminum foil lengthwise to fit into the bottom and up two opposite sides of the pan. (The foil handles will make

the brownie easy to remove from the pan.) Lightly butter the foil, dust the inside of the pan with flour, and tap out the excess flour.

2. Sift the flour, baking soda, and salt together into a medium bowl. Melt the butter in a medium saucepan over medium heat. Remove the saucepan from the heat. Add the chocolate and let it stand until it is softened, about 3 minutes. Whisk until the chocolate is smooth and melted. Add the brown sugar, granulated sugar, syrup, and vanilla and whisk until smooth. One at a time, add in the eggs, whisking well after each addition. Using a large wooden spoon, stir in the flour mixture. Stir in the walnuts. Spread the batter evenly in the baking pan.

3. Bake until a wooden toothpick inserted in the center of the brownie comes out with a moist crumb, 25 to 30 minutes. Let the brownie cool completely in the pan on a wire cake rack. Lift up on the foil handles to remove the brownie in one piece. Cut into 9 bars and serve. (The brownies can be stored in an airtight container at room temperature for up to 5 days.) ✍

Double-Chocolate Chip Cookies

The chocolate chip cookie assumed its exalted place in food history when it was invented by Ruth Wakefield, the owner of the Toll House Inn in Massachusetts (see page 100). True chocolate lovers will say this version, with chocolate dough, improves upon the original. This dough is soft, so chilling it briefly makes it easier to scoop. If you wish, substitute 1 cup (115 g) of coarsely chopped walnuts for an equal amount of the chocolate chips.

Cookie Monster's chocolate chip cookies are actually rice cakes painted with spots.

2 cups (260 g) all-purpose flour

¼ cup (20 g) cocoa powder, preferably Dutch-processed

1 teaspoon baking powder

½ teaspoon table salt

1 cup (225 g) unsalted butter, at room temperature

¾ cup (150 g) granulated sugar

¾ cup (150 g) packed light brown sugar

2 large eggs, at room temperature

1 teaspoon vanilla extract

2 cups (340 g) semisweet chocolate chips

1. Whisk together the flour, cocoa, baking powder, and salt in a medium bowl. Beat the butter, granulated sugar, and brown sugar together in a second medium bowl with an electric mixer set on medium-high speed until combined and pale, about 2 minutes. One at a time, beat in the eggs, beating well after each addition, followed by the vanilla. Using a wooden spoon, stir in the flour mixture. Stir in the chocolate chips. Cover and refrigerate the dough until lightly chilled, 30 minutes to 1 hour.

2. Position racks in the top third and center of the oven and preheat the oven to 375°F (190°F). Have ready two large rimmed baking sheets.

3. Using about 1 tablespoon for each cookie, drop the dough onto the ungreased baking sheets, spacing the mounds 2 inches (5 cm) apart. Bake, switching the positions of the sheets from top to bottom and front to back halfway through baking, until the cookies are barely beginning to brown around the edges, about 12 minutes. Do not overbake.

4. Let the cookies cool on the sheets for 5 minutes. Transfer them to a wire cake rack and let them cool completely. (The cookies can be stored in an airtight container at room temperature for up to 5 days.)

CHOCOLATE MACARONS

For a hundred years, the French macaron—two slightly domed meringue shells sandwiched together with ganache, buttercream, or preserves—was known only in France. Then, in the late 20th century, the exquisite cookie began to appear in macaron-only bakeries in North America, Japan, and other places around the world. While macarons come in a rainbow of colors and flavors, chocolate, of course, remains a favorite. Plan ahead; the egg whites need to be separated and chilled for at least 1 day in advance of baking. The ingredient amounts must be carefully calibrated and may be slightly off when translated to the American volume system, so weighing works best.

An MIT student taught a robot how to bake chocolate cookies.

MACARONS

8 large egg whites (200 g)

2¼ cups (200 g) almond flour (also called almond meal), preferably made from blanched almonds

3½ cups (350 g) confectioners' sugar

¼ cup (20 g) natural or Dutch-processed cocoa powder

¼ cup plus 2 teaspoons (60 g) granulated sugar

GANACHE

6 ounces (170 g) bittersweet (about 60 percent cacao) chocolate, finely chopped

¾ cup (180 mL) heavy cream

¼ cup (55 g) unsalted butter, at room temperature

1. **To make the cookies:** Refrigerate the egg whites, covered loosely with a paper towel, for 24 to 36 hours.

2. When ready to make the batter, transfer the egg whites to a grease-free large bowl, and let stand, uncovered, at room temperature for 2 hours.

3. Pulse the almond flour, confectioners' sugar, and cocoa in a food processor about 10 times, until well combined. (You may do this in batches.) Sift the mixture through a wire sieve into a large bowl, being sure to rub any coarse bits through the sieve. Transfer the mixture to a large bowl.

4. Whip the whites with an electric mixer on medium-high speed until they form soft peaks. Gradually beat in the granulated sugar and continue whipping the whites until they form very stiff and shiny peaks. If you turn the bowl upside down, the whipped whites should cling to the bowl. If not, beat longer.

5. Sift half of the almond mixture over the meringue and fold it in with a large spatula or balloon whisk. The meringue will deflate. Repeat with the remaining almond mixture to make a thick, homogeneous batter.

6. Line two 18-by-13-inch (46-by-33-cm) half-sheet pans with silicone baking mats or parchment paper. Transfer about half of the batter to a large pastry bag fitted with a ½-inch (12-mm) plain pastry tip. Pipe the batter on the baking sheets in 2½-inch (6-cm) rounds, spacing them about 2 inches (5 cm) apart, allowing 16 to 20 rounds for each baking sheet. Repeat with the remaining batter. Firmly rap the sheets a couple of times on the work surface to disperse any air bubbles inside the macarons. If peaks are visible on the macarons, pat them down with a fingertip dipped in water. Set the sheets aside at room temperature until a thin skin forms on the surface of the macarons and they are not tacky or sticky when touched, 20 minutes to 1 hour, depending on the weather (it will take longer on humid days).

7. Position a rack in the center of the oven and preheat the oven to 300°F (150°C). One sheet at a time, bake the macarons for 15 minutes. Rotate the baking sheet from front to back for even baking. Continue baking until the macarons are crisp and can be lifted gently from the sheet, about 10 to 15 minutes more. (They won't be truly easy to remove from the sheet until they have cooled.) Let the macarons cool completely on the sheet.

8. **To make the ganache:** Bring the cream to a simmer in a small saucepan over medium heat. Put the chocolate in a medium bowl. Pour in the hot cream and let stand for 3 minutes to soften the chocolate. Whisk until the ganache is smooth. Add the butter and whisk until it is absorbed. Refrigerate, stirring occasionally, until the ganache is firm enough to hold its shape when spooned, about 1 hour. Do not let the ganache cool until it is hard.

9. Transfer the ganache to a pastry bag fitted with a ½-inch (12-mm) opening. For each

cookie, pipe a generous tablespoon of the ganache onto the flat side of a macaron. Top with another macaron, flat sides facing each other. Gently press them together until the ganache oozes to the edge of the macaron "sandwich."

10. Transfer the macarons to a platter and cover with plastic wrap. Refrigerate for at least 8 hours and up to 5 days to allow the shells to soften. Remove the macarons from the refrigerator for 15 minutes before serving. ❧

Tips for Macaron Success

Macarons are famously temperamental, but even if your macarons aren't perfect (they should have crinkly bottoms called "feet" supporting smooth tops without any air spaces inside), they will still taste delicious. Below are some details that lead to baking success:

- Do not make macarons during humid weather unless you have a very efficient air conditioner in your kitchen.
- Resting the egg whites allows excess moisture to evaporate and makes for a firmer meringue batter. Be sure to bring the whites to room temperature before whipping them. The meringue should be very stiff and shiny.
- The almond flour must be dry and at room temperature. If your almond flour is refrigerated from storage, spread the flour out on a baking sheet and let it stand, uncovered, at room temperature, overnight to remove absorbed moisture.
- Process the almond flour with the sugar until it is very fine, and do not skip the sifting step. The almond flour mixture must have a delicate texture or the shells will be rough.

- For an excellent alternative dessert, make Eton Mess: Crush unfilled macarons and mix with whipped cream and fresh raspberries. The proportions aren't important.

BLACK FOREST CAKE

A masterpiece of German pastry, the Black Forest cake—Schwarzwälder Kirschtorte—
is named for the region that produces morello sour cherries. Used in cooking,
they are also distilled into *kirschwasser* ("cherry water" in German), a clear eau-
de-vie. Authentic kirsch is expensive because it takes 22 pounds of cherries
to make a liter. Domestic kirsch or rum can be used as substitutes. But Black
Forest cake is all about the three C's: cherries, chocolate, and cream. Cherries
and whipped cream are spread among three layers of chocolate cake with more
cherries and whipped cream on the top and sides.

German
Chocolate Cake
was invented in the
United States,
not Germany.

CHOCOLATE SPONGE CAKE

Softened butter and flour for the pan

¼ cup (60 g) unsalted butter

I teaspoon vanilla extract

4 large eggs, at room temperature

½ cup (100 g) granulated sugar

½ cup (65 g) cake flour

¼ cup (20 g) natural or Dutch-processed
cocoa powder

⅛ teaspoon table salt

One 24.7-ounce (700-g) jar pitted morello
cherries in light syrup

¼ cup (60 mL) kirsch or golden rum

2 tablespoons confectioners' sugar

WHIPPED CREAM

I envelope (about 2¼ teaspoons)
unflavored gelatin powder

2½ cups (600 mL) heavy cream

¼ cup (50 g) confectioners' sugar

I teaspoon vanilla extract

4 ounces (115 g) semisweet chocolate
(about 55 percent cacao), in one piece

8 maraschino cherries, drained and patted
dry

1. **To make the cake:** Position a rack in the center of the oven and preheat the oven to 350°F
(180°C). Lightly butter the bottom only of an

8-by-2-inch (20-by-5-cm) cake pan. Line the bottom with a round of waxed or parchment paper. Butter the waxed paper, dust it with flour, and tap out the excess flour. Do not butter or flour the sides of the pan.

2. Cook the butter in a small saucepan over medium heat until the butter is melted and boiling. Boil for 1 minute. Remove from the heat and let stand for 3 minutes. Skim off the foam from the surface and pour the butter into a ramekin or custard cup. Measure 3 tablespoons clarified butter (make up any missing butter with vegetable oil, if necessary) to a medium bowl. Add the vanilla.

3. Whisk the eggs and granulated sugar together in the bowl of a standing electric mixer or a large heatproof bowl. Place the bowl in a larger bowl of hot tap water. Whisk until the mixture is warm to the touch and the sugar is dissolved. Remove the bowl from the water. Using an electric mixer on medium-high speed, beat the egg mixture until it is very pale and has tripled in volume, about 4 minutes (or 6 minutes with a hand mixer).

4. Sift the cake flour, cocoa, and salt together onto a piece of waxed paper. Sift half of the flour mixture over the egg mixture and fold it in with a large rubber spatula until just a few streaks of the flour mixture remain visible, keeping the egg mixture as inflated

as possible. Repeat with the remaining flour mixture, leaving a few streaks of the flour mixture visible. Spoon about one-quarter of the batter into the butter mixture and fold them together until the butter is absorbed. Add the butter mixture to the remaining batter and fold until the batter is completely combined. Spread the batter evenly in the pan.

5. Bake until the cake springs back when lightly pressed in the center with a fingertip, 25 to 30 minutes. Cool the cake in the pan on a wire cake rack for 5 minutes. Run a knife around the inside of the pan. Invert the cake onto the cake rack, remove the pan, and peel off the paper. Turn the cake right side up and let it cool completely.

6. Drain the cherries well in a wire sieve over a medium bowl and reserve ⅔ cup (160 mL) of their syrup. Add the kirsch and confectioners' sugar to the syrup and whisk to dissolve the sugar. Spread the cherries on paper towels and pat to dry them well.

7. **To make the whipped cream:** Chill a large bowl in the refrigerator. Add 3 tablespoons cold water to a ramekin or custard cup. Sprinkle the gelatin evenly over the water and let it stand until the gelatin softens, about 5 minutes. Meanwhile, bring ¼ inch (6 mm) of water in a small skillet

to a simmer. Place the ramekin in the skillet. Using a small rubber spatula, stir the gelatin mixture until the gelatin is completely dissolved, at least 1 minute. Remove the ramekin from the skillet and stir in 2 tablespoons of the heavy cream.

8. Add the remaining heavy cream to the chilled bowl and add the confectioners' sugar and vanilla. Beat with an electric mixer on high speed just until the cream forms soft peaks. With the mixer running, beat in the gelatin mixture and mix just until stiff. Transfer about 1 cup (120 g) of the whipped cream to a pastry bag fitted with a ½-inch (12-mm) fluted pastry tip and set it aside.

9. Using a long serrated knife, cut the cake horizontally into three equal layers. Place one layer on an 8-inch (20-cm) cardboard cake round or the bottom of a tart pan. Brush about one-third of the cherry syrup over the layer. Using a flexible metal spatula, spread the layer with about 1 cup (120 g) of the whipped cream. Scatter half of the remaining cherries over the whipped cream. Repeat with a second layer, another third of the syrup, 1 cup (120 g) of the cream, and the remaining cherries. Top the cake with the layer and brush with the remaining syrup. Place the cake on a decorating turntable or an upturned mixing bowl with a wide, flat bottom. Spread the top, and then the sides, with the remaining cream. Do not worry if the frosting is a bit thin around the sides. Pipe 8 equally spaced rosettes around the top perimeter of the cake.

10. Using the large holes of a box grater, working on a sheet of waxed paper, grate about half of the chocolate into tiny curls. Holding the cake on the cardboard round, and working over a rimmed baking sheet, tilt the cake slightly and spoon and toss the chocolate onto the sides and around the top edge of the cake. (Don't touch the curls with your hands or the chocolate will melt.) Place a cherry in each rosette. Refrigerate, uncovered, for at least 2 hours and up to 2 days. Slice and serve chilled. ✎

THE EASIEST CHOCOLATE LAYER CAKE

With COCOA FROSTING

Many foods were rationed during World War II, so American homemakers had to come up with replacements when baking cakes. Mayonnaise cleverly contributes both eggs and oil to the batter, a technique worth using today. The coffee complements the chocolate by giving it just a hint of mocha flavor.

A WWII pilot called the Candy Bomber parachuted chocolates to German children below.

CAKE

Softened butter and flour, for the cake pans

2 cups (280 g) unbleached all-purpose flour (measure with dip-and-sweep method)

1 cup (200 g) granulated sugar

⅓ cup plus 1 tablespoon (30 g) natural cocoa powder (not Dutch-processed)

2 teaspoons baking soda

¼ teaspoon table salt

1 cup (110 g) mayonnaise

1 cup (240 mL) cold brewed coffee (not dark roast)

1 teaspoon vanilla extract

FROSTING

2½ cups (500 g) confectioners' sugar

⅔ cup (50 g) natural cocoa powder (not Dutch-processed)

6 tablespoons (85 g) unsalted butter, at room temperature

¾ cup (180 mL) heavy cream

1 teaspoon vanilla extract

1. **To make the cake:** Position a rack in the center of the oven and preheat the oven to 350°F (180°C). Lightly butter two round 8-by-1½-inch (20-by-4-cm) cake pans. Line the bottoms of the pans with waxed or parchment paper. Dust the insides of the pans with flour and tap out the excess flour.

2. Sift the flour, sugar, cocoa, baking powder, and salt together into a large bowl and make a well in the center. Whisk the mayonnaise, cold coffee, and vanilla together in another bowl. Pour the liquids into the well in the dry ingredients. Whisk just until the batter is smooth. Divide the batter evenly among the cake pans and smooth the tops with a metal icing spatula.

3. Bake until a wooden toothpick inserted in the center of the cakes comes out clean, 20 to 25 minutes. Cool the cakes in the pans on wire cake racks for 10 minutes. Run a dinner knife around the insides of the pans. Invert the cakes onto the racks to unmold and carefully remove the waxed paper. Let cool completely.

4. **To make the frosting:** Sift the confectioners' sugar and cocoa together into a medium bowl. Add the butter and mix with an electric mixer on low speed until crumbly. Gradually mix in the heavy cream until the frosting is smooth. Increase the speed to high and beat for a few seconds until the frosting is fluffy. Beat in the vanilla.

5. Place one cake layer upside down on a serving platter. Slip strips of waxed paper under the cake layer to protect the platter from the frosting. Using a metal icing spatula, spread about ¾ cup (200 g) of the frosting. Top with the second cake layer, right side up. Evenly frost the top and sides of the cake with the remaining frosting. Remove the waxed paper. (The cake can be refrigerated for up to 1 day. Let the cake stand at room temperature for 1 hour before serving.)

FINE CHOCOLATE GÂTEAU
With CRÈME ANGLAISE

Here is a Canadian chocolate cake in the French style, as befits a dessert from the historic Fortress of Louisbourg, a living history museum in Nova Scotia. The Mars family tree has some roots in Canada, and it is said that this single-layer cake was a particular favorite of Forrest Mars. The gâteau is so dense, moist, and fudgy that it resembles a confection as much as a cake. Be sure to let it chill at least 8 hours before serving so it can set completely.

This cake is especially good when made with American Heritage Chocolate, which is based on a recipe from the American colonial period. You can purchase this chocolate at select American historical sites. For the locations (some of which will mail the chocolate), go to http://www.americanheritagechocolate.com/home/merchants.

In the 1700s, French-Canadian privateers targeted British ships for their cacao cargo.

CAKE

Softened butter and flour, for the pan

1 pound (455 g) bittersweet chocolate (about 60 percent cacao) or American Heritage Chocolate

1¼ cups (285 g) unsalted butter, cut into tablespoons

7 large eggs, at room temperature

1¼ cups (250 g) sugar

1½ teaspoons vanilla extract

1 cup (130 g) unbleached all-purpose flour

½ teaspoon table salt

½ teaspoon ground cinnamon, optional

CRÈME ANGLAISE

1½ cups (360 mL) whole milk

1 vanilla bean, split lengthwise, or 1 teaspoon vanilla extract

4 large egg yolks, at room temperature

¼ cup (50 g) sugar

(or, if using a hand mixer, about 5 minutes). Reduce the heat to low. Add the chocolate mixture and mix until combined. Remove the bowl from the stand. Sift the flour, salt, and cinnamon, if using, over the chocolate mixture and fold it in with a flexible spatula. Spread the batter evenly in the pan.

1. **To make the cake:** Position a rack in the center of the oven and preheat the oven to 350°F (180°C). Butter and flour the inside of a 9-by-3-inch (23-by-7.5-cm) springform pan, tapping out the excess flour.

2. Melt the butter in a large saucepan over low heat. Remove the saucepan from the heat. Add the chocolate and let stand to soften the chocolate, about 3 minutes. Whisk until the chocolate is smooth and melted. Let the mixture cool until tepid but still liquid, about 10 minutes.

3. Combine the eggs, sugar, and vanilla in a large bowl and beat with an electric mixer on high speed until the mixture is very pale and tripled in volume, about 3 minutes

4. Bake until the center is set and the batter moves as a unit when the pan is gently shaken, about 35 minutes. Let the gâteau cool completely in the pan on a wire cake rack.

5. Run a knife around the inside of the pan and remove the sides. Wrap the gâteau with plastic wrap and refrigerate until completely chilled, at least 8 hours or preferably 24 hours. (The gâteau can be refrigerated for up to 3 days.)

6. **To make the crème anglaise:** Heat the milk with the vanilla bean halves in a medium saucepan over low heat until small bubbles form around the edges of the milk, about 10 minutes. Remove the vanilla bean halves. Using the tip of a small sharp knife, scrape the tiny seeds from the halves into the milk, and discard the halves.

7. Whisk the yolks and sugar together in a medium heatproof bowl until the mixture is pale and thickened. Gradually whisk in the hot milk. Return the entire mixture to the saucepan. Cook the custard, stirring constantly with a wooden spoon, until the custard thickens and coats the spoon (a finger drawn through the custard on the spoon will cut a swath) and reads 185°F (85°C) on an instant-read thermometer. Strain the custard through a wire sieve into a clean medium heatproof bowl. If using vanilla extract, stir it in now. Cover the bowl loosely with plastic wrap. Let the sauce cool, stirring occasionally, until tepid, about 1 hour. Cover the bowl tightly with plastic wrap and refrigerate until chilled, at least 2 hours. (The crème anglaise can be refrigerated for up to 2 days.)

8. To serve, let the cake stand at room temperature for 1 hour. Using a thin knife dipped into hot water, slice the gâteau. For each serving, spoon a few tablespoons of the crème anglaise onto a dessert plate, and top with a slice of the gâteau. ❧

Tips for Keeping Chocolate Fresh

Chocolate can be stored for several months with little risk of damage. However, if it is stored improperly or for too long, the cocoa butter in the chocolate can become rancid, or the sugar crystals can become unstable, which affects the taste and texture of the chocolate.

- To store bar chocolate, wrap it in foil and then in plastic. Keep it in a cool, dark place, such as a basement or a high cupboard. Dark chocolate can be stored for up to one year. In milk chocolate and white chocolate, the milk's butterfat breaks down and turns rancid, so these chocolates can be stored for only four to six months.
- Improperly stored chocolate develops chocolate bloom. Fat bloom—white streaks and blotches—develops when chocolate is stored in a warm environment. When there is too much moisture present, the chocolate will feel a little rough, which is a sign of sugar bloom.
- Although bloom does not render the chocolate inedible, it must be tempered again to retrieve its gloss and texture. If you are planning to melt and chop the chocolate for baking, go right ahead. Cake, cookies, ice cream, or pie will be just fine.

SACHER TORTE

Sacher torte is the chocolate-glazed symbol of Vienna's passion for pastries. It has a long history, going back to the 1830s, when a young baker, Franz Sacher, invented it. Over time, Franz prospered, and the cake became the specialty of his family's hostelry. More than a hundred years after the sweet's inception, there was a bitter lawsuit between the Sacher Hotel and Demel, the famous bakery to which Franz's grandson defected and brought the "original" recipe. It took more than seven years for the court to come to a Solomon-like decision, allowing both places to include slightly different forms of "Sacher" in their cake names. The cake is supposed to be firm, and in fact each delicious bite should be moistened with a bit of the whipped cream that is always served on the side.

One study found that chocolate melting in your mouth can cause a more intense "buzz" than kissing.

CAKE

Softened butter and flour, for the pan

5 ounces (140 g) semisweet chocolate (about 55 percent cacao), finely chopped

½ cup plus 1 tablespoon (130 g) unsalted butter, at room temperature

1 cup (100 g) confectioners' sugar

6 large eggs, separated, at room temperature

1 teaspoon vanilla extract

½ cup (100 g) granulated sugar

1 cup (130 g) unbleached all-purpose flour

One 12-oz (340-g) jar apricot preserves (1 cup)

2 tablespoons dark rum or water

CHOCOLATE ICING

1 cup (200 g) granulated sugar

4 ounces (110 g) semisweet chocolate (about 55 percent cacao), finely chopped

1 tablespoon unsalted butter

WHIPPED CREAM FOR SERVING

1 cup (240 mL) heavy cream

2 tablespoons confectioners' sugar

1 teaspoon vanilla extract

1. **To make the cake:** Position a rack in the center of the oven and preheat to 350°F (180°C). Lightly butter the inside of a

9-by-3-inch (23-by-7.5-cm) springform pan. Line the bottom with a round of parchment or waxed paper. Dust the sides of the pan with flour and tap out the excess flour.

2. Place the chocolate in a heatproof bowl. Bring ½ inch (12 mm) of water to a simmer in a small skillet and turn off the heat. Put the bowl in the water and let stand, stirring often, until the chocolate has melted. Remove the bowl from the water and let the chocolate stand, stirring occasionally, until it is cool but still fluid.

3. Beat the butter and confectioners' sugar together in a medium bowl with an electric mixer on medium-high speed until the mixture is light in color and texture, about 3 minutes. One at a time, beat in the yolks, scraping down the sides of the bowl

as needed. Add the cooled chocolate and the vanilla and mix until combined.

4. Using clean beaters, whip the whites in a large bowl with an electric mixer on high speed until soft peaks form. Gradually beat in the granulated sugar until the eggs form shiny peaks. Using a rubber spatula, stir about one-fourth of the beaten whites into the chocolate mixture to lighten it. Fold in the remaining whites, leaving a few visible wisps of whites. Sift half of the flour over the mixture, and fold it in. Repeat with the remaining flour.

5. Spread the batter evenly in the pan. Bake until a toothpick inserted in the center comes out clean, about 45 minutes. (The cake will dome slightly.) Let the cake cool in the pan on a wire cake rack for 10 minutes. Run a dinner knife around the insides of the pan and remove the sides. Carefully invert the cake onto the rack and discard the paper. Turn the cake right side up and let it cool completely.

6. Meanwhile, bring the preserves and rum to a boil in a small saucepan over medium heat. Cook, stirring often, until the bubbles are large, about 2 minutes. Rub the preserves through a wire sieve into a small bowl, discarding the solids in the sieve.

7. Using a long serrated knife, trim and level the top of the cake, reserving the crumbs. Cut the cake in half horizontally. Place one cake layer on an 8-inch (20-cm) cardboard round, and return to the wire rack, set over a large rimmed baking sheet. Brush the top of the cake layer with some of the apricot glaze. Place the second cake layer on top and brush the top and sides of the stacked cake with the remaining glaze, being sure to fill any air holes in the cake layer with the glaze and the reserved crumbs. Let cool to set the apricot glaze.

8. **To make the chocolate icing**: Combine the sugar, chocolate, butter, and ½ cup (120 mL) water in a small heavy-bottomed saucepan and attach a candy thermometer. Stirring often, bring the mixture to a boil over medium-high heat. Reduce the heat to medium and cook, without stirring, until the icing reaches the soft-ball stage at 234°F (112°C), about 5 minutes. Let the icing cool slightly, without stirring, for 3 to 5 minutes.

9. Pour the warm chocolate icing on top of the cake. Do not scrape the dregs out of the saucepan, or the icing will be streaky. Using an offset metal spatula, gently smooth the icing over the cake, allowing it to run down the sides and being sure that the icing completely coats the cake (patch any bare spots with the spatula and the icing under the rack). Let the icing cool until it is just set, about 30 minutes. Transfer the cake to a serving platter. Refrigerate until the icing is completely set, at least 1 hour. (The cake can be refrigerated for up to 1 day.) Remove the cake from the refrigerator about 1 hour before serving.

10. **To whip the cream**: Whip the cream, confectioners' sugar, and vanilla in a chilled medium bowl with an electric mixer set on high speed just until soft peaks form. (The cream can be covered and refrigerated for up to 1 day. If it separates, whisk briefly before serving.)

11. To serve, slice with a sharp knife dipped into hot water. Transfer each slice to a dessert plate and add a large dollop of whipped cream. ✒

CHOCOLATE TRES LECHES CAKE

Hailing from Latin America, *tres leches* ("three milks" in Spanish) cake has established itself as one of the most beloved of all desserts in the Latino kitchen. The cake is soaked and moistened with canned condensed and evaporated milks and topped with whipped cream (these are the three milks) to keep the cake from becoming stale too quickly in a dry, hot environment. Here is a chocolate version that is even better than the original.

In 2013, scientists invented meltproof chocolate to make it more popular in warm climates.

CAKE

Unsalted butter, for the pan

¾ cup (100 g) unbleached all-purpose flour, plus more for the pan

¼ cup (20 g) Dutch-processed or natural cocoa powder

I teaspoon baking powder

¼ teaspoon table salt

⅓ cup (80 mL) whole milk

I teaspoon vanilla extract

5 large eggs, at room temperature

¾ cup (150 g) granulated sugar

SOAK

One 14-ounce (393-g) can sweetened condensed milk

One 12-ounce (336-g) can evaporated milk

½ cup (50 g) confectioners' sugar

TOPPING

1½ cups (360 mL) heavy cream

¼ cup (25 g) confectioners' sugar

I teaspoon vanilla extract

4 ounces (115 g) white chocolate, in one piece

1. **To make the cake:** Position a rack in the center of the oven and preheat to 350°F (180°C). Lightly butter the inside of a 13-by-9-inch (32.5-by-22.5-cm) baking pan, dust it with flour, and tap out the excess flour.

2. Sift the flour, cocoa, baking powder, and salt together into a bowl. Mix the milk and vanilla in the milk's measuring cup. Whisk the eggs and granulated sugar together in the bowl of a standing mixer a large heatproof bowl. Place the bowl in a larger bowl of hot tap water. Stir with a whisk until the mixture is warm to the touch and the sugar is dissolved. Remove the bowl from the water.

3. Using an electric mixer on high speed, beat the egg mixture until it is very pale and has tripled in volume, about 4 minutes (or 6 minutes with a hand mixer). Reduce the speed to low. In three additions, beat in the flour mixture, alternating with two equal additions of the milk mixture, and mix the batter until smooth, scraping down the sides of the bowl as needed. Spread the batter evenly in the pan.

4. Bake until the top of the cake springs back when lightly pressed in the center with a fingertip, about 30 minutes. Cool the cake in the pan on a wire cake rack for 10 minutes.

5. **To make the soaking mixture**: Whisk the condensed and evaporated milks together in a bowl.

Pierce the cake all over with a meat fork. In two or three additions, pour the soaking milk mixture evenly over the warm cake in the pan, letting the first addition soak into the cake before adding another. Cool completely. Cover with plastic wrap and refrigerate until chilled, at least 2 hours. (The cake can be refrigerated for up to 36 hours.)

6. **To make the topping**: Whip the cream, confectioners' sugar, and vanilla in a chilled medium bowl with an electric mixer on high speed until stiff. Spread evenly over the chilled cake. Using a vegetable peeler, press hard on the white chocolate block to shave curls over the cake. Slice into equal portions and serve chilled. ❧

CHOCOLATE-PEANUT EMPANADAS

This recipe celebrates the Latin American origin of chocolate with a sweet empanada, an individual hand-pie popular throughout the continent. Empanadas are most often filled with savory ingredients, but here both pastry and filling are sweet. While you can eat these with your hands, they can also be served warm on plates and topped with a scoop of ice cream.

It takes about 400 cacao beans to make one pound of chocolate.

FILLING

- ¼ cup (60 mL) heavy cream
- 2 ounces (55 g) semisweet chocolate (about 55 percent cacao), finely chopped
- 2 tablespoons chunky peanut butter
- 2 tablespoons finely chopped unsalted peanuts

DOUGH

- 1 cup (130 g) unbleached all-purpose flour, plus more for rolling out the dough
- 2 tablespoons granulated sugar
- 1 teaspoon baking powder
- ⅛ teaspoon table salt
- ½ cup (115 g) cold unsalted butter, cut into ½-inch (12-mm) cubes
- ¼ cup (60 mL) heavy cream
- 1 tablespoon ice water
- 2 teaspoons cider vinegar
- 1 large egg yolk
- 1 tablespoon heavy cream
- 2 tablespoons finely chopped unsalted peanuts
- Dulce de leche or vanilla ice cream, for serving
- Confectioners' sugar, for garnish

1. **To make the filling:** Bring the cream to a simmer in a small saucepan over medium

heat. Put the chocolate in a small bowl. Add the hot cream and let the mixture stand until the chocolate has softened, about 3 minutes. Add the peanut butter and whisk until the mixture is smooth. Whisk in the peanuts. Cover with plastic wrap and refrigerate until the filling is chilled and firm, at least 1 and up to 8 hours.

2. **To make the dough**: Whisk the flour, sugar, baking powder, and salt together in a medium bowl. Add the butter and cut it in with a pastry blender until the mixture resembles coarse crumbs with some pea-size pieces of butter. Mix the cream, ice water, and vinegar together. Pour into the flour mixture and stir until the mixture clumps together. Gather up into a thick disk. Wrap the dish in plastic wrap and refrigerate until chilled but pliable, about 1 hour.

3. Using a dessert spoon, divide the filling into six equal portions and shape each into a rough log about 2 inches (5 cm) long. Refrigerate the logs to keep them chilled.

4. Cut the dough into six equal portions. One at a time, on a lightly floured work surface, roll out the dough into a 6-inch (15-cm) round. Using a saucer as a template, cut out a 5-inch (12-cm) round, discarding the trimmings. On a plate, stack the dough rounds, separating them with pieces of waxed paper, and refrigerate for 15 to 30 minutes.

5. Meanwhile, position a rack in the center of the oven and preheat the oven to 375°F (190°C). Line a large rimmed baking sheet with parchment paper.

6. Beat the egg yolk and cream together in a ramekin to combine. Place a pastry disk on the work surface. Place a chocolate log on the bottom third of the disk, about 1 inch (2.5 cm) from the bottom edge. Using a pastry brush, lightly brush the bottom half of the disk along its edge with the yolk mixture. Fold the disk in half from top to bottom to enclose the log, press the open edges closed with the tines of a fork, and pierce the top of the empanada once. Place the empanadas on the baking sheet. Brush the tops lightly with some of the yolk mixture and sprinkle with the peanuts.

7. Bake until the empanadas are golden brown, about 20 minutes. Let the empanadas cool on the baking sheet for at least 20 minutes (be sure the filling is warm, not hot). To serve, place an empanada on a dessert plate, add a scoop of ice cream, and sift the confectioners' sugar on top. Serve immediately. ✒

CHAMPURRADO

This Mexican version of hot chocolate is especially popular during the Christmas season. The texture gets its body from masa harina, the main ingredient in tortillas, and the drink should be whisked well before serving to give it a foamy topping. Try to use Mexican chocolate for its authentic sweet and spicy flavor. This beverage may be an acquired taste for American palates.

Hot cocoa is made with cocoa powder; hot chocolate is prepared with shavings of solid chocolate.

⅓ cup (35 g) masa harina (see Note)
2 cups (480 mL) whole milk
1 disk (90 g) Mexican chocolate (see Note), coarsely chopped

1. Whisk the masa harina with 2 cups (480 mL) water in a medium saucepan to dissolve the masa. Whisk in the milk and add the chocolate. Bring to a boil over medium heat, whisking almost constantly. Reduce the heat to low and let the mixture simmer until lightly thickened, about 1 minute. Remove from the heat and whisk vigorously until the mixture is foamy. Ladle into cups and serve hot.

2. Note: Masa harina is made from corn treated with the mineral lime. Cinnamon-laced Mexican chocolate (Abuelita and Ibarra are widely available brands) is shaped into disks, wrapped in paper, and specifically manufactured to use in making hot chocolate or *champurrado*. Three ounces (85 g) of Baker's Sweet Chocolate with a pinch of ground cinnamon is a good substitute. ✣

MISSISSIPPI MUD PIE

Some recipes for this classic have ice cream, some have marshmallows, some have chocolate syrup, and some are cakes cooked in a pie tin. Here's a version that no one will quibble with: real chocolate pudding in a chocolate and pecan crust, topped with whipped cream.

The scent of chocolate in a bookstore made customers more likely to buy cookbooks.

CRUST AND GARNISH

Softened butter, for the pan

1 cup (85 g) coarsely crushed chocolate graham crackers

½ cup (55 g) coarsely chopped pecans

2 tablespoons granulated sugar

3 tablespoons unsalted butter, melted

PUDDING

3 cups (720 mL) whole milk

5 large egg yolks

¼ cup (35 g) cornstarch

⅔ cup (130 g) granulated sugar

Pinch of table salt

4 ounces (115 g) semisweet chocolate (about 55 percent cacao), finely chopped

2 tablespoons unsalted butter

1 teaspoon vanilla extract

TOPPING

1¼ cups (300 mL) heavy cream

2 tablespoons confectioners' sugar

1 teaspoon vanilla extract

1. **To make the crust and garnish:** Position a rack in the center of the oven and preheat the oven to 350°F (180°C). Lightly butter the inside of a 9-by-1½-inch (23-by-4-cm) pie pan.

2. Combine the graham cracker crumbs, pecans, and granulated sugar in a food processor and pulse about 10 times until the pecans are finely chopped. Add the melted butter and pulse to combine. Transfer ¼ cup (35 g) of the crumb mixture to a small bowl, cover, and set aside at room temperature for the garnish.

Press the remaining crumb mixture firmly and evenly into the pan.

3. Bake until the crust smells sweet and toasty, 10 to 15 minutes. Let cool completely on a wire cake rack.

4. **To make the filling**: Whisk ½ cup (120 mL) of the milk with the yolks and cornstarch in a medium heatproof bowl until well combined. Heat the remaining 2½ cups (600 mL) of milk with the granulated sugar and salt in a medium heavy-bottomed saucepan over medium heat until the mixture is simmering. Gradually whisk the hot milk mixture into the yolk mixture, then return the entire mixture to the saucepan. Cook over medium heat, stirring constantly, until the mixture comes to a full boil. Reduce the heat to low and let the custard boil for 30 seconds to cook completely. Strain it through a wire sieve into a clean medium bowl. Add the chocolate, butter, and vanilla and let stand until the chocolate softens, about 3 minutes. Whisk the mixture until smooth.

5. Pour the filling into the cooled crust and smooth the top. Cover with a piece of plastic wrap pressed directly onto the surface and pierce a few holes in the wrap with the tip of a small knife to allow steam to escape. Let cool until tepid, about 30 minutes. Refrigerate until the filling is chilled and set, at least 2 hours or up to 2 days.

6. **To make the topping**: Whip the cream, confectioners' sugar, and vanilla together in a chilled medium bowl with an electric mixer until stiff. Uncover the pie and spread the whipped cream over the filling. Refrigerate until ready to serve, up to 8 hours. Just before serving, sprinkle the reserved crumb mixture over the topping. Slice and serve chilled. 🍃

Chocolate-Raspberry Silk Tart

While Brussels is famous for its luxurious sweetshops, just about every Belgian community has a fine local chocolatier. Belgium carefully regulates its economically important chocolate industry to allow only the very best ingredients (for example, forbidding any vegetable fats and controlling the amount of cacao mass in the chocolate). Here is a beautiful dessert that looks as if it came from a Belgian bakery, although it is simple enough to make at home, especially because the sweet tart dough is pressed into a pan rather than rolled out.

The Brussels airport sells more chocolate than any other venue in the world.

DOUGH

I cup plus I tablespoon (140 g) unbleached
   all-purpose flour

3 tablespoons sugar

¼ teaspoon table salt

6 tablespoons (85 g) cold unsalted butter,
   cut into tablespoons

I large egg yolk, lightly beaten

FILLING

I½ cups (360 mL) heavy cream

9 ounces (255 g) bittersweet chocolate (about
   62 percent cacao), coarsely chopped

3 tablespoons (45 g) unsalted butter,
   at room temperature

2 tablespoons golden syrup or light corn syrup

I tablespoon raspberry-flavored liqueur,
   such as Chambord

½ cup (120 g) raspberry preserves (optional)

3 cups fresh raspberries, about three
   6-ounce (170-g) containers

1. **To make the crust:** Position a rack in the center of the oven and preheat the oven to 350°F (180°C).

2. Meanwhile, pulse the flour, sugar, and salt together in a food processor. Add the butter and pulse about 15 times, or until the mixture resembles fine crumbs. Pour in the yolk and pulse just until the dough clumps together. (Or whisk the flour, sugar, and salt together in a medium bowl. Add the butter. Using a pastry blender, cut the butter into the flour mixture with a pastry blender until the mixture resembles fine crumbs. Stir in the yolk and mix until the dough clumps together.) Gather up the dough and press it firmly and evenly into the bottom and up the sides of a 9-inch (23-cm) round tart pan with a removable bottom. Prick the dough all over with a fork. Freeze the dough-lined pan for 15 to 30 minutes.

3. Line the pan with aluminum foil and fill with pie weights or dried beans. Bake until visible edges of the dough look set, about 15 minutes. Lift up and remove the foil with the weights. Continue baking until the pastry is golden brown, about 10 minutes more.

Let the pastry cool completely in the pan on a wire cake rack.

4. **To make the filling:** Heat the cream in a small saucepan over medium heat until simmering. Put the chocolate in a medium heatproof bowl. Pour the hot cream over the chocolate and let the mixture stand to soften the chocolate, about 3 minutes. Add the butter, syrup, and liqueur and whisk until the chocolate is melted and smooth. Pour the filling into the cooled pastry. Cover the tart loosely with plastic wrap and refrigerate until the filling is set, about 2 hours.

5. **To make the optional glaze:** Bring the preserves and 1 tablespoon water to a boil in a small saucepan over medium heat, stirring

often. Let it boil for 1 minute. Strain the preserves through a wire sieve into a small bowl, discarding the solids. Cool slightly.

6. Arrange the raspberries, rounded sides up, closely together in concentric circles on the filling. Using a pastry brush, coat the berries with the glaze, if using. Chill for 5 minutes to set the glaze. (The tart can be refrigerated for up to 1 day.) Slice and serve chilled. 🍃

Tips for Choosing Your Chocolate

Different taste preferences and recipes call for different kinds of chocolate. Here are some helpful hints for choosing the chocolate that suits your palate or your desired dessert.

- If the label on chocolate shows a high percentage of cacao (sometimes called cocoa), that means the bar has a higher proportion of cacao to sugar. When there is a lower percentage of cacao, the chocolate contains less cacao beans and more sugar, and will therefore taste sweeter.
- The terms "bittersweet" and "semisweet" are broadly used. In the United States, both can have cacao content ranging from 35 percent to 88 percent.
- If you like bitter, almost mouth-puckering chocolate, look for bars with higher than 65 percent cacao. It's not unusual to find bittersweet (dark chocolate) bars that are 71 or 75 percent cacao.
- Most of the recipes in this book were tested with moderately bitter chocolate (about 55 percent). If the cacao content is not designated, you can assume that the chocolate falls into this category.

- Unsweetened chocolate contains no sugar and is used in classic recipes, such as brownies.
- Picking the right chocolate is much like selecting the perfect wine for drinking or for cooking. It requires trial and error. Now you have a good excuse to taste a lot of different chocolates!
- Never substitute milk chocolate for dark chocolate in recipes. The proteins in the milk chocolate are heat sensitive, and it contains less chocolate liquor than dark chocolate. The recipe will be unbalanced and unsuccessful.
- White chocolate also contains delicate dairy proteins that are difficult to melt smoothly, so it is most often used by home bakers as an accent. Shavings might be scattered over the top of a cake, or chips can be folded into cookie batter along with semisweet chocolate morsels.

Chocolate-Ginger Mochi

The Japanese have developed a passion for chocolate. Small, round, and chewy, mochi are made from sweet rice flour or pounded glutinous rice and are filled with various sweet ingredients, ranging from ice cream to lotus paste. Here they are filled with a truffle-like chocolate mixture.

Sweet rice flour is milled from a very starchy variety of rice and is used specifically for making mochi and other desserts. Be sure to purchase sweet rice flour and not standard rice flour.

Serve mochi with cups of hot green tea.

In Japan, women gift Giri-choco (obligation chocolate) to their male colleagues, bosses, and friends on Valentine's Day.

FILLING

½ cup (120 mL) heavy cream

6 ounces (170 g) semisweet chocolate (about 55 percent cacao), finely chopped

1 tablespoon ginger liqueur or ginger-flavored beverage syrup

MOCHI

1 cup sweet white rice flour, plus more for dusting

2 cups (400 g) granulated sugar

2 tablespoons cocoa powder, preferably Dutch-processed

2 tablespoons confectioners' sugar

1. **To make the filling:** Bring the cream to a simmer in a small saucepan over medium heat. Put the chocolate in a small heatproof bowl. Add the hot cream and let stand for 3 minutes to soften the chocolate. Add the liqueur and whisk until the chocolate is smooth and melted. Cover the bowl with plastic wrap and refrigerate until chilled and firm, at least 2 and up to 8 hours.

2. **To make the mochi:** Place a steamer rack in a large saucepan. Add enough water to the saucepan to come almost to the bottom of the rack. Cover tightly and bring to a boil over high heat.

3. Put the rice flour in a medium heatproof bowl. Gradually stir in enough cold water, about ¾ cup (180 mL), to make a smooth dough. Cover the bowl tightly with plastic wrap. Place the bowl on the steamer rack. Reduce the heat to medium so the water simmers steadily, and cover the saucepan tightly. Steam for 20 minutes or until the rice flour mixture is firmer, but still soft. Remove the bowl from the saucepan. Carefully remove the plastic (watch out for the steam). In thirds, stir in the granulated sugar, stirring well after each addition to melt the sugar.

4. Dust the work surface well with rice flour. Scrape the hot dough out onto the work surface. Coat your hands with rice flour and shape the hot dough, folding it over on itself, into a smooth cylinder about 14 inches (35.5 cm) long. The dough will be hot at first, but it will cool rapidly.

5. Using a melon baller, scoop out 12 equal portions of the chocolate filling and shape them into balls. Clean and dry your hands.

6. Cut the rice flour cylinder into 12 equal portions. Coat your hands again with rice flour. Working with one piece

at a time, flatten a dough portion under the heel of your hand into a 3½-inch (9-cm) diameter round, with the edges of the round thinner than the center. Place a chocolate ball in the center of the round. Bring up the edges of the round to enclose the ball and pinch the seams shut. With cupped palms, shape the dough into a half-sphere shape with a flat bottom. Place the mochi, rounded side up, on a small baking sheet. Sift the cocoa and confectioners' sugar through a wire sieve over the mochi, and gently roll them in the cocoa mixture to coat. The mochi can be stored at cool room temperature, loosely covered with plastic wrap, for up to 2 days. Do not refrigerate the mochi. 🍃

CHOCOLATE TIFFIN
With RAISINS AND WALNUTS

From the United Kingdom, tiffin was originally made with leftover digestive biscuits and whatever sweet fruits were around until someone had the idea to add chocolate. Tiffin is one of the easiest treats to make since it's literally a mash-up of cookies, chocolate, dried fruit, and nuts. Feel free to substitute other fruits, nuts, or cookies as you wish.

The Quakers were pioneers of English chocolate manufacturing.

½ cup (115 g) unsalted butter, thinly sliced

3 tablespoons golden syrup, light corn syrup, or honey

5 ounces (140 g) coarsely chopped semi-sweet chocolate

5 ounces (140 g) coarsely chopped milk chocolate

1 cup (65 g) coarsely crushed digestive cookies (such as McVitie's) or graham crackers

1 cup (140 g) seedless raisins, preferably golden

1 cup (115 g) coarsely chopped walnuts

1. Line an 8-inch (20-cm) square baking dish with plastic wrap, letting the excess wrap hang over the sides.

2. Combine the butter and syrup together in a large heatproof bowl. Place over a large saucepan of very hot, but not simmering, water, and let the mixture melt, stirring often. Add the semisweet and milk chocolates and stir occasionally until the mixture is smooth and the chocolate is melted. Remove the bowl from the saucepan.

3. Stir the graham crackers, raisins, and walnuts into the chocolate mixture. Scrape the mixture into the baking dish. Fold the plastic wrap over to cover the top, and press it gently to smooth out the surface. Refrigerate the tiffin until it is firm, about 2 hours.

4. Invert and unmold the tiffin onto a chopping board and discard the plastic wrap. Using a large knife, cut the tiffin into 9 equal squares. Serve chilled or at room temperature. (The tiffin can be refrigerated in a covered container for up to 2 weeks.) 🍃

Tips for Melting Chocolate

Chocolate needs to be melted with dry, gentle heat. If the chocolate is overheated, or comes into direct contact with even a drop of water or steam, it will thicken into a clump—a sad phenomenon call seizing. Seized chocolate cannot be saved and must be discarded. So, when melting chocolate, temperature and moisture control are primary concerns. You can melt chocolate on the stove top or in the microwave. A microwave does not require water and removes the danger of seizing the chocolate, it is important to use moderate power to avoid overheating.

Stove Top:
- Use a heatproof bowl that fits snugly over a saucepan.
- Bring about 1 inch (2.5 cm) water to a bare simmer in the saucepan over medium heat. Then reduce the heat to its lowest setting.
- Put the chopped chocolate in the bowl. Do not cover the bowl.
- Melt the chocolate, stirring occasionally with a dry wooden spoon or rubber spatula until smooth.

Microwave:
- Put the chopped chocolate in a microwave-safe bowl. Do not cover the bowl.
- Microwave the chocolate in 30-second intervals at medium (50 percent) power. After each interval, stir the chocolate with a dry wooden spoon or rubber spatula. (It may not look melted until you stir it.)
- Continue microwaving the chocolate just until it is melted and smooth. Do not overheat the chocolate.

CHOCOLATE-COGNAC TRUFFLES

Chocolate truffles are perfect for making at home because their rough look is part of their charm. They supposedly resemble an actual truffle, a fungus that grows underground, and so the clinging cocoa resembles "dirt." This traditional recipe is especially useful because you can change the flavor by substituting other liqueurs or beverage flavorings for the rum (for example, crème de menthe to create mint truffles or Grand Marnier for orange). The deliciously creamy filling is enrobed with a thin coating of chocolate before being rolled in cocoa. Keep truffles refrigerated until just before serving.

The chocolate in this recipe is tempered, a process of melting, heating, and cooling chocolate to specific temperatures in order to retain the chocolate's shine and texture. If you don't want to do this procedure, just melt all of the chocolate in the usual manner (see page 181), and then let it cool until it is tepid but still liquid. If the chocolate is too warm, it will melt the filling. Without tempering, the chocolate will look dull, but it will still taste good.

The chocolate company founded by the prime minister of the UAE fills truffles with camel milk, a regional delicacy.

FILLING

⅓ cup (80 mL) heavy cream

2 tablespoons unsalted butter

8 ounces (225 g) bittersweet chocolate (about 62 percent cacao), coarsely chopped

2 tablespoons cognac, brandy, or favorite beverage flavoring syrup

4 ounces (115 g) bittersweet chocolate (about 62 percent cacao), finely chopped

2 tablespoons Dutch-processed cocoa powder

1. Bring about ½ inch (12 mm) of water to a simmer in a small skillet. Reduce the heat

to very low. Combine the heavy cream and butter in a medium heatproof bowl. Place the bowl in the skillet and heat, stirring often, until the butter has melted. Add the coarsely chopped chocolate and remove the bowl from the skillet. Let the mixture stand until the chocolate softens, about 3 minutes. Whisk until it is melted and smooth, about 3 minutes. Whisk in the cognac.

2. Let the mixture cool until it is tepid. Tightly cover the bowl with plastic wrap and refrigerate until chilled and firm, at least 2 hours and up to 8 hours.

3. Using a melon baller or dessert spoon, allowing about a tablespoon for each truffle, scoop up the truffle mixture and shape it into a rough ball. Place the truffles on a plate. Loosely cover with plastic wrap and refrigerate or freeze until chilled and firm, about 30 minutes. The truffles must be very cold for coating.

4. Return the water in the skillet to simmering and reduce the heat to very low. Put about three-quarters (90 g) of the finely chopped chocolate in a clean medium heatproof bowl. Place the bowl in the skillet and heat, stirring often, until the chocolate is melted and smooth and reads about 120°F (49°C) on an instant-read thermometer. (Tilt the bowl so the chocolate pools to get an accurate reading.)

5. Remove the bowl from the water. Add the remaining finely chopped chocolate and stir until it is melted and smooth. Set the melted chocolate aside and let it stand, stirring occasionally, until it is cooled to 90°F (32°C) on the thermometer (tilting the bowl to get an accurate reading) and slightly thickened, about 5 minutes.

6. Line a small baking sheet or plate with parchment or waxed paper. Place the chilled truffles on the work surface. One at a time, drop a truffle into the chocolate. Immediately pick up the truffle—it will have chocolate on one side—and transfer it to your palm. Quickly roll the truffle in your palm to spread the chocolate over the truffle in a very thin layer. This should only take a few seconds. Place the coated truffle on the lined baking sheet. (Do not coat the truffle with so much chocolate that it makes "feet" when placed on the baking sheet.) Refrigerate the truffles, uncovered, until the chocolate coating is set, about 30 minutes.

7. Sift the cocoa over the truffles and toss them to coat. Loosely cover the truffles with plastic wrap and refrigerate for up to 5 days. Serve chilled or at room temperature. ✎

Tips for Making Perfect Truffles

To get the most out of your truffles, experiment with different flavorings, and store them properly. Using high-quality chocolate is also particularly worthwhile.

How to Make Flavorful Ganache

- To flavor the ganache, infuse the hot cream with the fruit, herbs, spices, liqueur, or coffee.
- Warm ganache will separate in the refrigerator, so let it cool to room temperature before chilling it.

Coating Your Truffles

- Achieving an even coating of hard chocolate is made easy with the hand method in this recipe. Note that this is not the classic enrobing technique that creates a smooth shell around a filling. You want to see the rough edges of a chocolate truffle, as this simulates the look of a real truffle.
- Keep a skillet with about ½ inch (12 mm) of hot water over low heat on hand. If the melted chocolate thickens and becomes too cool for dipping, immerse the bottom of the bowl into the water for about ten seconds to warm it. Then remove it and stir until it returns to its former consistency.

How to Store Your Truffles

- Chocolate truffles are best when eaten fresh, or within two to three days of making.

- For longer-term storage, truffles can be frozen for two to three months. Wrap them in plastic and then pop them in an airtight container or sealable plastic bag.
- Before eating, let the truffles thaw overnight in the refrigerator. The next day, unwrap them and let them come to room temperature before serving. Coat the truffles with extra cocoa, if needed.

CHOCOLATE-COFFEE FLAN

Flan, a rich custard baked in a caramel-lined container, represents one of Spain's finest culinary contributions, especially when combined with chocolate and coffee. Flan must be made a few hours before serving so it has a chance to become firm, which makes it perfect for entertaining.

A study found that countries that consume more chocolate have more Nobel Prize winners.

1⅓ cups (265 g) sugar

1 cup (120 mL) heavy cream

1 cup (120 mL) whole milk

One 3-inch (7.5-cm) cinnamon stick

4 ounces (115 g) extra-bittersweet chocolate (about 70 percent cacao), coarsely chopped

4 large eggs, at room temperature

1 teaspoon vanilla extract

1. Position a rack in the center of the oven and preheat the oven to 325°F (165°C).

2. Combine 1 cup (200 g) of the sugar with ¼ cup (60 mL) water in a small saucepan. Bring the mixture to a boil over high heat, stirring constantly with a wooden spoon to help dissolve the sugar. Stop stirring and boil, swirling the saucepan by its handle and brushing down any sugar crystals that form on the side of the pan with a pastry brush dipped in water, until the caramel is lightly smoking and the color of a new penny, 3 to 5 minutes.

3. Immediately pour equal amounts of the caramel into six 6-ounce (180-mL) ramekins. Using a kitchen towel to protect your fingers, tilt each ramekin to coat the inside with caramel. If the caramel solidifies, warm the ramekin in the oven to warm the caramel for about 2 minutes, then continue.

4. Heat the cream, milk, and cinnamon stick in a medium saucepan over medium-low heat until the mixture is simmering. Remove the saucepan from the heat. Add the chocolate and let the mixture stand until the chocolate softens, about 3

minutes. Whisk until the chocolate is melted and smooth. Discard the cinnamon stick.

5. Whisk the eggs, remaining ⅓ cup (65 g) sugar, and vanilla together in a medium heatproof bowl until pale yellow. Gradually whisk in the warm chocolate mixture. Strain the mixture through a wire sieve into a 1-quart (950-mL) liquid measuring cup or pitcher. Pour equal amounts of the mixture into the ramekins.

6. Place the ramekins in a large roasting pan. Pour enough hot tap water to come about ½ inch (12 mm) up the sides of the ramekins.

Cover the roasting pan with aluminum foil. Carefully slide the pan into the oven. Bake until a dinner knife inserted in the center of a flan comes out clean, about 45 minutes. Uncover the pan and let the flans stand for 5 minutes. Remove from the water and let them cool, about 1 hour. Cover each with plastic wrap and refrigerate until chilled, at least 4 hours and up to 2 days.

7. For each serving, run a dinner knife around the inside of a ramekin. Cover with a dessert plate, and invert the plate and ramekin together to unmold the flan with the caramel onto the plate. Serve chilled. ✍

Mocha Chip Ice Cream Pie

With HOT FUDGE SAUCE

A true hot fudge sauce pours in a warm stream and firms up to a chewy consistency when it hits cold ice cream, while chocolate syrup is thinner and pours more freely. Hot fudge sauce is basically fudge that is undercooked and never allowed to set into candy. No one is quite sure about how or where hot fudge came about, but it's a good bet that someone somewhere undercooked some fudge and discovered a new sauce. Here it is served with a coffee-and-chocolate ice cream pie as an update of the American hot fudge sundae.

Approximately 70 percent of the world's cacao is now grown in Africa.

CRUST AND FILLING

Softened butter, for the pie pan
Chocolate Crust (page 172)
1 quart (0.95 L) coffee ice cream
½ cup (85 g) miniature semisweet
 chocolate chips

SAUCE

1 cup (100 g) granulated sugar
2 tablespoons natural or Dutch-processed
 cocoa powder
1 cup (240 mL) heavy cream
¼ cup (60 mL) light corn syrup or
 corn syrup
⅛ teaspoon cider or distilled white vinegar

2 ounces (55 g) unsweetened chocolate,
 finely chopped
2 tablespoons unsalted butter
1 teaspoon vanilla extract

WHIPPED CREAM AND GARNISH

Whipped Cream (page 163), for garnish
24 chocolate-covered espresso beans,
 for garnish

1. **To make the pie:** Position a rack in the center of the oven and preheat to 350°F (180°C). Lightly butter a 9-by-1½-inch (23-by-4-cm) pie pan.

2. Press the crust mixture firmly and evenly into the pan. Bake until crust looks set and smells toasty, 12 to 15 minutes. Let cool completely on a wire cake rack.

3. Soften the ice cream slightly at room temperature. Add the mini chocolate chips and mix them in with a large spoon or spatula. Spread the mixture the cooled crust. Cover the pie with plastic wrap and freeze until the ice cream is firm, at least 4 and up to 24 hours.

4. **To make the sauce:** Whisk the sugar and cocoa together in a heavy-bottomed medium saucepan. Whisk in about half of the cream to make a paste. Add the remaining cream with the syrup and vinegar and whisk until combined. Add the chocolate and butter. Attach a candy thermometer to the saucepan. Bring to a boil over high heat, stirring constantly. Reduce the heat to medium and cook, stirring often, until the sauce reaches

234°F (112°C), or the soft-ball stage (a teaspoon of the sauce, dropped into a small glass of ice water, will solidify enough that it can be shaped into a soft and pliable ball), about 5 minutes. Stir in the vanilla. Transfer to a medium heat-proof bowl. Let the sauce cool until tepid but pourable, 20 to 30 minutes. (The sauce can be cooled, covered, and refrigerated for up to 5 days. Reheat, stirring often, in a saucepan over low heat.)

5. **To make the whipped cream:** Whip the cream, confectioners' sugar, and vanilla in a chilled medium bowl with an electric mixer set on high speed until stiff peaks form. (The cream can be refrigerated for up to 4 hours. If it separates, whisk before using.)

6. Transfer the whipped cream to a pastry bag fitted with a ½-inch (12-mm) open star tip. Pipe 8 equally spaced rosettes around the perimeter of the pie. Top each with 3 espresso beans. Slice the pie, transfer each portion to a dessert plate, top with a few spoonfuls of the warm sauce, and serve immediately. ⤠

Chocolate Mousse

For decades, chocolate mousse was one of the classic desserts offered at French restaurants throughout the world. A dessert cart with a fruit tart, individual ramekins of crème caramel, and a cut-glass bowl of chocolate mousse was rolled up to the table by a waiter wearing a tuxedo. He spooned a serving of chocolate mousse into a stemmed glass and topped it with plenty of whipped cream. Voilà! Chocolate mousse has since become the ultimate chocolate dessert for make-ahead entertaining. This excellent update uses cooked, instead of raw, egg yolks and is just as smooth, creamy, and decadent as the old-school version.

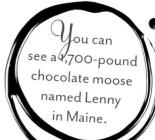

You can see a 1,700-pound chocolate moose named Lenny in Maine.

4 large egg yolks
4 tablespoons granulated sugar
1½ (360 mL) cups heavy cream

½ cup (120 mL) whole milk
6 ounces (170 g) semisweet chocolate
   (about 55 percent cacao), finely chopped
2 tablespoons dark rum, cognac, or
   brewed coffee
1 teaspoon vanilla extract
Whipped cream (page 163), for serving

1. Whisk the yolks and 2 tablespoons of the sugar together in a medium heatproof bowl until the mixture is pale and thickened. Bring ½ cup (120 mL) of the cream and the milk to a simmer in a medium heavy-bottomed saucepan over medium heat.

Gradually whisk the hot cream mixture into the yolk mixture. Return the entire mixture to the saucepan.

2. Cook the custard, stirring constantly with a wooden spoon, until the custard thickens and coats the spoon (a finger drawn through the custard on the spoon will cut a swath) and reads 185°F (85°C) on an instant-read thermometer. Strain the custard through a wire sieve into a clean medium heatproof bowl. Add the chocolate and let stand until the chocolate softens, about 3 minutes. Whisk well until the chocolate melts and the mixture is smooth. Whisk in the rum and vanilla.

3. Place the bowl in a larger bowl of iced water and let it stand, whisking occasionally, until the chocolate mixture is cool and thickened, but not set, about 20 minutes. Remove the bowl from the ice water.

4. Using an electric mixer, whip the remaining 1 cup (240 mL) cream and 2 tablespoons sugar in a chilled medium bowl until soft peaks form. Stir about one-fourth of the whipped cream into the cooled chocolate mixture, then fold in the remaining whipped cream. Divide evenly among six individual ramekins or glasses. Cover with plastic wrap and refrigerate until chilled, at least 2 hours or up to 2 days.

5. To serve, top each mousse with a dollop of whipped cream and serve chilled. 🍃

CHOCOLATE TIRAMISU

Tiramisu appeared in northern Italy in the 1970s and spread like wildfire to dessert menus all over the world. This concoction of soaked ladyfingers and creamy mascarpone usually has just a dusting of cocoa on top, but this version has lots of chocolate flavor in every bite. Make it at least a few hours ahead to allow the flavors time to mingle.

Red wine generally pairs best with dark chocolate, sweet sparkling wine pairs with white.

½ cup (50 g) confectioners' sugar

2 tablespoons natural or Dutch-processed cocoa

Two 8- to 8.8-ounce (455- to 500-g) containers mascarpone

1 cup (240 mL) cool brewed coffee

¼ cup (60 mL) white or dark crème de cacao, dark rum, or chocolate-flavored syrup

About 24 Italian-style ladyfingers (*savoiardi*)

½ cup (85 g) mini semisweet chocolate chips

Homemade Chocolate Syrup (page 197)

1. Sift the confectioners' sugar and cocoa together into a medium bowl. Add the mascarpone and heavy cream. Using a rubber spatula, mix and mash the mixture together until it is smooth and combined.

2. Mix the coffee and crème de cacao together in a liquid measuring cup. Pour half of the coffee mixture into a shallow bowl. One at a time, quickly dip half of the ladyfingers into the syrup (do not soak them) and arrange them side by side in an 11-by-8½-inch (28-by-21.5-cm) baking dish, breaking them to fit as needed. Spread half of the mascarpone mixture over the ladyfingers. Repeat with the remaining ladyfingers (drizzle any remaining coffee mixture over the ladyfingers), coffee mixture, and mascarpone mixture. Sprinkle the mini chips on top.

3. Cover the dish with plastic wrap and refrigerate until chilled, at least 4 hours. (The tiramisu can be refrigerated up to 2 days ahead.)

4. Cut the tiramisu into 8 to 10 equal portions and transfer to individual dessert plates. Drizzle each serving with chocolate syrup, and serve chilled. ☙

Homemade Chocolate Syrup

True chocolate fans should have a jar of this homemade chocolate syrup on hand in the refrigerator to use at a whim. For a chocolate beverage, stir 2 to 3 tablespoons of the syrup into 1 cup (240 mL) of hot or cold milk. Use it as a dessert sauce, spooned over ice cream or cake. Or, if no one's looking, enjoy the syrup by the spoonful straight from the container.

According to legend, Giacomo Casanova drank chocolate before his romantic trysts.

1 cup (200 g) sugar
½ cup (40 g) natural cocoa powder
Dash of table salt
1 teaspoon vanilla extract

1. Whisk the sugar, cocoa, and salt together in a small heavy-bottomed saucepan. Gradually whisk ¾ cup (180 mL) of the water to dissolve the cocoa mixture. Bring to a boil over medium heat, whisking often. Reduce the heat to medium-low and cook at a brisk simmer until the syrup is reduced to about 1¼ cups (300 mL).

2. Transfer the syrup to a container and let it cool completely. (The syrup can be covered and refrigerated for up to 3 weeks.) ✍

CHICKEN
With MOLE SAUCE

Mole, one of the classic Mexican sauces, has only about an ounce of chocolate, but even this small amount is indispensable. It balances the disparate ingredients (including sweet raisins, warm cinnamon) with its gentle bitterness. As mole recipes go, this one is notable for its simplicity and can be made with supermarket ingredients. Chicken and mole are the most common combination, but you can also use mole with shrimp, pork, or fish. Rice is a good side dish for mole, and be sure to serve with a pile of tortillas to sop up the sauce.

In Oaxaca, Mexico, children drink chocolate in the morning to ward off scorpion and bee stings.

3 tablespoons olive oil

1 medium yellow onion, chopped

2 garlic cloves, chopped

3 tablespoons pure ground ancho chili or chili powder

Pinch of ground cinnamon

⅛ teaspoon freshly ground black pepper

2 cups (480 mL) canned reduced-sodium chicken broth

1 cup (225 g) seeded and chopped ripe plum tomatoes or drained canned plum tomatoes

¾ cup (100 g) seedless raisins

¼ cup (35 g) salted peanuts

1 ounce (30 g) unsweetened chocolate, finely chopped

Kosher salt

2 tablespoons olive oil, plus more for the baking dish

6 chicken breast halves with skin and bone, 10 to 12 ounces (285 to 340 g) each

1½ teaspoons kosher salt

½ teaspoon freshly ground black pepper

1 teaspoon sesame seeds, for garnish

boil, stirring occasionally. Remove from the heat. Add the chocolate and stir until it melts into the sauce. (The sauce can be cooled, covered, and refrigerated for up to 1 day. Reheat over low heat, stirring often.)

1. Heat 1 tablespoon of the oil in a medium skillet over medium heat. Add the onion and garlic and cook, stirring occasionally, until the onion is translucent, about 4 minutes. Add the ground chili, cinnamon, and pepper and mix well. Stir in the broth, tomatoes, and raisins and bring the mixture to a boil. Reduce the heat to medium-low and simmer, uncovered, until the broth has reduced by about one-fourth, about 20 minutes. Remove from the heat and let the mixture cool until it is tepid.

2. Stir in the peanuts. In batches, puree the sauce mixture in a blender and transfer it to a bowl. Clean the skillet. Heat the remaining 2 tablespoons of oil in the skillet over medium heat. Add the sauce (be careful, as it will splatter) and bring to a

3. Position a rack in the center of the oven and preheat to 400°F (200°C). Lightly oil a 10-by-15-inch (25-by-38-cm) baking dish.

4. Heat the oil in a large skillet over medium-high heat. Season the chicken all over with the salt and pepper. In batches, without crowding, add the chicken to the skillet, skin side down, and cook until the skin is browned, about 5 minutes. Transfer the chicken, skin side up, to the baking dish.

5. Bake the chicken for 30 minutes. Pour the mole around the chicken, leaving the skin exposed. Continue baking until an instant-read thermometer inserted in the thickest part of a breast not touching a bone reads 165°F (74°C), about 15 minutes. Let stand for 5 minutes. Sprinkle the sesame seeds over the chicken with mole and serve hot. 🥄

KUNA CACAO AND BANANA DRINK

The Kuna people, who live on islands off the coast of Panama and in a number of Colombian villages, drink many cups of cacao every day. The bitter beverage is made with dried and ground cacao beans. Here is a sugarless recipe made with cacao nibs and banana. Use a soft, ripe banana that is well spotted with brown marks, but not a squishy, black one.

The Kuna's cacao-rich diet has been linked to strong cardiovascular health.

¼ cup (35 g) cacao nibs
1 ripe banana, cut into chunks
Honey or agave nectar (optional)

1. Pulse the cacao nibs with 1 cup (240 mL) water in a blender until the nibs are finely chopped. Pour into a medium saucepan and add 3 cups (720 mL) water and the banana. Bring to a boil over high heat. Reduce the heat to low and simmer, stirring often, for 10 minutes. Strain the mixture through a wire sieve into a heatproof medium bowl, mashing the banana. Discard the solids in the sieve. If you wish, sweeten the drink with honey or agave. Ladle into cups and serve hot. 🍃

American Heritage Hot Chocolate

Mars Chocolate North America has created American Heritage™ Chocolate according to a colonial American ingredient list dating from the 1750s, which includes a touch of chili and spices such as orange peel, anise, nutmeg, and vanilla. It makes a thick and flavorful hot chocolate, and can be mixed with either milk or water. (The American forefathers would have used the latter.)

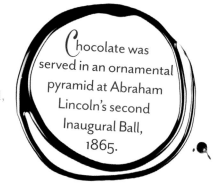

Chocolate was served in an ornamental pyramid at Abraham Lincoln's second Inaugural Ball, 1865.

½ cup (120 mL) whole milk or water
One 6-ounce (170-g) package American Heritage Chocolate, very finely chopped (see Note)

1. Bring the milk to a simmer in a small saucepan over medium heat. Remove from the heat. Add the chocolate and let stand until softened, about 1 minute. Whisk the mixture well until the chocolate is melted and the hot chocolate is foamy. Ladle into cups and serve.

2. Note: You can substitute 1⅓ cups (180 g) of American Heritage Hot Chocolate Drink Mix for the chopped chocolate. ✍

Tips for Chocolate Tasting

If you want to discover the chocolates you like best, it's fun to try different chocolates and make taste comparisons. Even better, invite some good friends to join you and turn your tasting into a party.

Start with five different brands and kinds of chocolate—perhaps one milk chocolate, two bittersweet, and two semisweet, or whatever suits your palate.

Before You Begin

- Grab a pen and paper for note-taking.
- Make sure the chocolate is at room temperature.
- Cleanse your palate. Plan the tasting for a few hours before or after a meal. Eat a few slices of apple or a plain unsalted cracker, or drink tepid water.
- Break the chocolate into quarter- to half-ounce pieces.

Smell

- Chocolate may have a deep dark chocolate aroma or a slightly mellower one. Its scent may have hints of herbs, flowers, fruit, vanilla, etc. Smell a piece of chocolate and take notes about its distinct scents.
- Break the piece in two and smell it at the break. Rub a small piece between your fingertips to release volatile aromatic components. The aromas you noticed before you broke the chocolate probably will be more pronounced.
- Close your eyes and concentrate on the aromas: sweet, earthy, herbal, floral . . .

Taste

- Put a small piece of chocolate on your tongue and let it melt.
- Concentrate on the sensation and how it's coating your tongue: smooth and light, or heavy and grainy?
- Note the tastes that come to mind. Are they fruity, bitter, sweet, or very intensely "chocolate"?
- Let the chocolate sit on your tongue for 30 to 60 seconds longer and notice how the flavors develop: If it is fruity, what kind of fruit do you taste? If it tastes floral, do you detect a particular flower?

The Finish

- Swallow the chocolate and wait for 20 to 30 seconds. Notice the finish: Is it clean and pleasant or slightly metallic? Does it linger nicely or is the aftertaste sweet and cloying?
- Cleanse your palate again. Jot down notes. Then pick up the next piece of chocolate and start again!

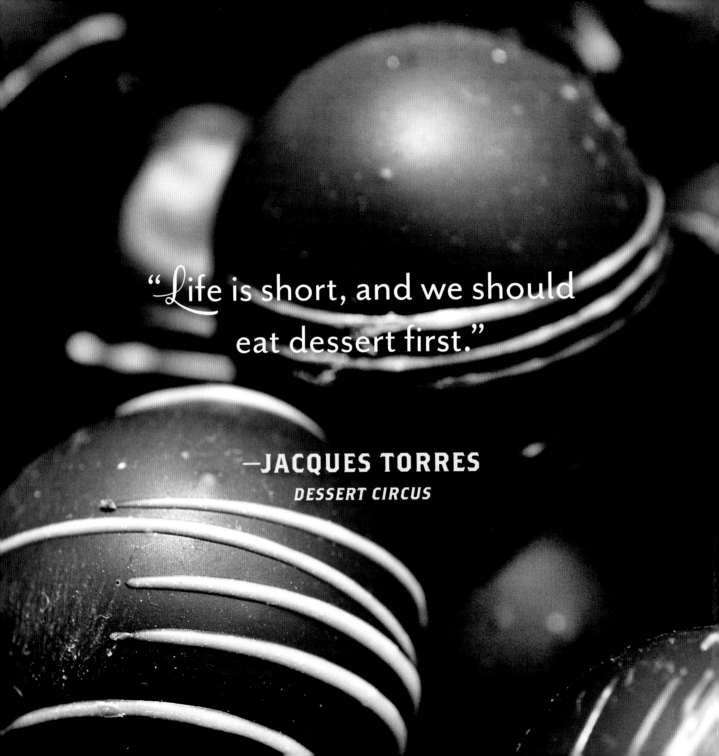

"Life is short, and we should eat dessert first."

—JACQUES TORRES
DESSERT CIRCUS

ACKNOWLEDGMENTS

More than 4.5 million farmers are involved with cacao farming worldwide. For decades Mars, Incorporated, has worked to bring prosperity to the farmers. Leading this effort has been Plant Sciences: the Mars Center for Cocoa Science—Barro Preto, Bahia, Brazil, with Claudio Dessimoni, Joao Leone, John Hammerstone, and Jean-Philippe Marelli; the Mars Cocoa Research Center—Tarrenge, Indonesia, with Smilja Lambert and Hussin Purung; the Mars Global Plant Science and Technology Research and Development Laboratory—Miami, Florida, with Ray Schnell and Juan Carlos Motomayor; and Vision for Change—Soubre, Côte d'Ivoire, with Andrew Harner, Josef Toledano, and Christophe Kouame. These groups are backed up by dozens more scientists and technicians globally working to deliver a sustainable supply chain of cacao. They are growing the future.

Special thanks to Robin Terry-Brown, senior editor, National Geographic Books, who guided this process with extraordinary grace; to the design and photo team, Moira Haney, Melissa Farris, and Katie Olsen; and to editorial assistants Michelle Cassidy and Moriah Petty. Additional thanks go to Gail Broadright of Mars, Incorporated; Alan Nathan; and Sedra Shapiro.

ILLUSTRATIONS CREDITS

Cover: (UPLE), Carol Sharp/http://www.flowerphotos.com/Eye Ubiquitous/Corbis; (UPRT), © 2015 Francesco Tonelli, Creative Director Laura Rosenberg; (LOLE), Man carrying a cacao pod, 1440-1521 (volcanic stone with traces of red pigment), Aztec/Brooklyn Museum of Art, New York, USA/Museum Collection Fund/Bridgeman Images; (LORT and Dove Bar, Front & Back), NGS Photographers Becky Hale and Mark Thiessen; (Foil Wrapper, Front & Back), nilsz/iStockphoto. Back Cover: (UPLE), Diana Taliun/Shutterstock; (UPRT), Angelo Cavalli/Alamy; (LOLE), Courtesy of Mars, Inc.; (LORT), HERA FOOD/Alamy.

1, MIB Pictures/Getty; 2-3, Zack Burris; 4, Anna Quaglia/Alamy; 6, StockFood/Stacy Ventura; 8, Kenneth Garrett; 9, Zack Burris; 10, Nigel Cattlin/Alamy; 11 (UP), Carol Sharp/http://www.flowerphotos.com/Eye Ubiquitous/Corbis; 11 (LO), amphotos/Alamy; 12, Francesco Tonelli/Alamy; 13, Francesco Tonelli; 14, Hulton Archive/Getty; 15, John Block/Getty; 16, Dennis Gottlieb/Getty; 18-19, Corbis; 21, Album/Art Resource, NY; 22, StockFood/Studio R. Schmitz; 23, Oksana Bratanova/Shutterstock; 24, DeAgostini//Getty; 25, North Wind Picture Archives/Alamy; 26-7, StockFood/Flávio Coelho; 28, StockFood/Ulrike Koeb; 29, Koraysa/Shutterstock; 30, Maxime Iattoni; 32-3, Gianni Dagli Orti/The Art Archive at Art Resource, NY; 34, Peter Titmuss/Alamy; 35, Yulia Davidovich/Shutterstock; 36-7, RMN-Grand Palais/Art Resource, NY; 38, Courtesy of Holl's Chocolates; 39, Tarker/Corbis; 41, The New York Public Library/Art Resource, NY; 42, The Granger Collection, NYC; 44-5, rvlsoft/iStockphoto; 46-7, Courtesy of Mount Vernon Ladies' Association; 48, The Gallery Collection/Corbis; 49, RMN-Grand Palais/Art Resource, NY; 50, © Boston Athenaeum, USA/Bridgeman Images; 51, NGS/Becky Hale and Mark Thiessen; 52, Angelo Cavalli/Alamy; 53, The Print Collector/Getty; 54, NGS/Becky Hale and Mark Thiessen; 55, Garsya/Shutterstock; 57, StockFood/Frank Adam; 58-9, © larus larus/500px Prime; 60, Amoret Tanner Collection/The Art Archive at Art Resource, NY; 61, Stuart Minzey/Getty; 63, David W. Hamilton/Getty; 64, Jeff Morgan 01/Alamy; 65, Carolyn Jenkins/Alamy; 66, margouillatphotos/iStockphoto; 67, HERA FOOD/Alamy; 68, StockFood/Howard Shooter; 70, milanfoto/iStockphoto; 71, Danielle Wood/cultura/Corbis; 72, StockFood/Heath Robbins; 74, imageBROKER/Alamy; 75, Mediablitzimages/Alamy; 76, Chronicle/Alamy; 77, Amiel/photocuisine/Corbis; 78-9, biffspandex/Getty; 80, Topical Press Agency/Getty; 81, Canadian Anglo-Boer War Museum; 82-3, Courtesy of Hershey Community Archives, Hershey, PA; 84 & 85, Courtesy of Mars, Inc.; 86, Courtesy of Jon Williamson; 87, StockFood GmbH/Alamy; 88, Courtesy of Mars, Inc.; 90, The New York Historical Society/Getty; 91, HERA FOOD/Alamy; 92-3, Travel Pictures/Alamy; 95, Mary Evans Picture Collection/Peter & Dawn Cope Collection/Everett Collection, Inc.; 96, Corbis; 97, D. Hurst/Alamy; 98-9, Sveta615/iStockphoto; 100, Seton Rossini; 101, StockFood/Alison Miksch; 102, RSBPhoto/Alamy; 103, Courtesy of Mars, Inc.; 104, incamerastock/Alamy; 105, AP Photo/U.S. Signal Corps; 106, Mary Evans/Retrograph Collection/Everett Collection; 108, leezsnow/iStockphoto; 109, AP Photo; 110-11, bgwalker/Getty; 112, Everett Collection; 113, Picsfive/Shutterstock; 115, SandraD Photography/Getty; 116, Everett Collection; 117, Mark Weinberg/Offset; 118-19, Adam Gault/Getty; 120-121, Calvin Chan/Alamy; 123, Norman Chan/Shutterstock; 124-5, NASA; 126-7, PLAINVIEW/iStockphoto; 128, Howard Sachs/Keystone/CNP/Getty; 129, DNY59/iStockphoto; 131, Richard Levine/Alamy; 132, StockFood/Jim Norton; 133, Jewel Samad/AFP/Getty; 134, photomaniauk/Alamy; 135, CAMERA PRESS/Clara Molden/Telegraph/Redux; 136-7, StockFood/Tim Imri; 138, NGS/Becky Hale and Mark Thiessen; 139, fcafotodigital/iStockphoto; 141, World Cocoa Foundation; 142, FotografiaBasica/iStockphoto; 144, small_frog/Getty; 145, HERA FOOD/Alamy; 146, masa44/Shutterstock; 147, Bon Appetit/Alamy; 148, StockFood/Ira Leoni; 151, Sergey Sklezznev/Shutterstock; 152, StockFood/Foodcollection; 155, StockFood/Foodcollection; 156, StockFood/Element Photo; 157, Andrew Scrivani/The New York Times/Redux Pictures; 158, NGS/Becky Hale and Mark Thiessen; 160, Viktoria Gavrilina/Shutterstock; 162, StockFood/Gräfe & Unzer Verlag/Wolfgang Schardt; 164, Lasse Kristensen/Shutterstock; 165, Africa Studio/Shutterstock; 167, NGS/Becky Hale and Mark Thiessen; 168, NGS/Becky Hale and Mark Thiessen; 171, Danicek/iStockphoto; 173, StockFood/Frank Wieder; 174, Bon Appetit/Alamy; 175, StockFood/Fotofood; 176, MaraZe/Shutterstock; 179, NGS/Becky Hale and Mark Thiessen; 181, NGS/Becky Hale and Mark Thiessen; 182, StockFood/Ruth Küng; 185, David J. Green-food themes/Alamy; 187, F. Hammond/Photocuisine/age fotostock; 188, NGS/Becky Hale and Mark Thiessen; 189, stockcam/iStockphoto; 191, StockFood/Susan Brooks-Dammann; 192, StockFood/Fotofood; 193, Brian Hagiwara/Getty; 194, NGS/Becky Hale and Mark Thiessen; 196, StockFood/Richard Jung Photography; 197, Anton Starikov/Alamy; 198, StockFood/Dominic Perri; 200, StockFood/Eising Studio—Food Photo & Video; 202, D7INAMI7S/Shutterstock; 203, spinetta/Shutterstock; 204-205, Abraham Nowitz/Getty.

GREAT MOMENTS IN CHOCOLATE HISTORY

Howard-Yana Shapiro

Published by the National Geographic Society

Gary E. Knell, *President and Chief Executive Officer*

John M. Fahey, *Chairman of the Board*

Declan Moore, *Chief Media Officer*

Chris Johns, *Chief Content Officer*

Prepared by the Book Division

Hector Sierra, *Senior Vice President and General Manager*

Lisa Thomas, *Senior Vice President and Editorial Director*

Jonathan Halling, *Creative Director*

Marianne R. Koszorus, *Design Director*

Robin Terry-Brown, *Senior Editor*

R. Gary Colbert, *Production Director*

Jennifer A. Thornton, *Director of Managing Editorial*

Susan S. Blair, *Director of Photography*

Meredith C. Wilcox, *Director, Administration and Rights Clearance*

Staff for This Book

Harriet Bell, *Project Editor*

Mary Goodbody, *Writer*

Jennifer Seidel, *Text Editor*

Rick Rodgers, *Recipe Developer*

Melissa Farris, *Art Director*

Moira Haney, *Illustrations Editor*

Laura Lakeway, *Contributing Illustrations Editor*

Patrick J. Bagley, *Assistant Illustrations Editor*

Katie Olsen, *Designer*

Carol Stroud, *Researcher*

Michelle Cassidy, Moriah Petty, *Editorial Assistants*

Carl Mehler, *Director of Maps*

Marshall Kiker, *Associate Managing Editor*

Judith Klein, *Senior Production Editor*

Rock Wheeler, *Rights Clearance Specialist*

Will Cline, *Production Manager*

Nicole Miller, *Design Production Assistant*

Darrick McRae, *Manager, Production Services*

Wendy Smith, *Imaging*

The National Geographic Society is one of the world's largest nonprofit scientific and educational organizations. Founded in 1888 to "increase and diffuse geographic knowledge," the member-supported Society works to inspire people to care about the planet. Through its online community, members can get closer to explorers and photographers, connect with other members around the world, and help make a difference. National Geographic reflects the world through its magazines, television programs, films, music and radio, books, DVDs, maps, exhibitions, live events, school publishing programs, interactive media, and merchandise. *National Geographic* magazine, the Society's official journal, published in English and 38 local-language editions, is read by more than 60 million people each month. The National Geographic Channel reaches 440 million households in 171 countries in 38 languages. National Geographic Digital Media receives more than 25 million visitors a month. National Geographic has funded more than 10,000 scientific research, conservation, and exploration projects and supports an education program promoting geography literacy. For more information, visit www.nationalgeographic.com.

For more information, please call 1-800-NGS LINE (647-5463) or write to the following address:

National Geographic Society
1145 17th Street NW
Washington, D.C. 20036-4688 U.S.A.

For information about special discounts for bulk purchases, please contact National Geographic Books Special Sales: ngspecsales@ngs.org

For rights or permissions inquiries, please contact National Geographic Books Subsidiary Rights: ngbookrights@ngs.org

Library of Congress Cataloging-in-Publication Data

Yana-Shapiro, Howard.
 Great moments in chocolate history : with 20 classic recipes from around the world / Howard Yana-Shapiro.
    pages cm
 ISBN 978-1-4262-1498-1 (hardcover : alk. paper)
 1. Cooking (Chcolate) 2. Chocolate--History--Chronology. 3. Chocolate industry--History--Chronology. I. Title.
 TX767.C5Y36 2015
 641.6'374--dc23
                                  2015012825
Printed in Hong Kong

15/THK/1

MARS

Around the world every day our more than 75,000 Mars Associates live our Five Principles—Quality, Responsibility, Mutuality, Efficiency and Freedom—that span across geographies, languages, cultures and generations.

The growth of our business is strongly linked to the way we tackle challenges in our supply chain. By sourcing sustainably we help to ensure the security of our raw materials and aim to improve the incomes of farmers who supply us. As an example, our *Vision for Change* project in Africa's Côte d'Ivoire which is the world's largest producer of cacao, brings farmers training, the tools they need to grow higher productivity cacao and build their individual prosperity.

We have partnered with companies, universities and government researchers to sequence, assemble and annotate the genome of the cacao plant as well as leading a global effort to map the genome of the peanut. These developments are not only critical for our products they are also important innovations for our industry, which is why we continue to share our research publicly for the use of scientists around the world. As a result of this work, new varieties of cacao will soon be released, increasing yield potential to build a more prosperous future for our industry.

Everyone has a favorite Mars chocolate brand. We love chocolates too, but we are about much more than just chocolate. We make all kinds of food, drinks, gum and confections, and have a large petfood and petcare business. Our over 115 brands owe their success to this strong foundation. They bring many moments of joy to millions of people and pets around the world.

Visit our website at www.mars.com to learn more about our business, how we are living sustainability, and why Mars is such a great place to work.

Follow Mars: facebook.com/mars, twitter.com/marsglobal, youtube.com/mars, linkedin.com/company/mars.